Administrative Feedback:
Monitoring Subordinates' Behavior

HERBERT KAUFMAN
with the collaboration of Michael Couzens

It sometimes seems that the heads of public agencies have little idea what their subordinates are doing. If this is so, much of administrative theory and practice becomes a myth, and real leadership cannot exist.

This book reports on a study of administrative feedback from subordinates to leaders in nine federal bureaus. It describes the processes by which information about subordinates flows back to headquarters and assesses that information in an effort to find out whether leaders could, if they want to, learn what happens below. With the feedback at their disposal, is it possible for them to determine what goes on at lower levels?

The findings confirm some conventional lore, but they also include some surprises. In particular, they indicate that increasing the volume of administrative feedback is unlikely to increase the leaders' knowledge of subordinate behavior; indeed, it may cause troublesome problems. To improve knowledge, the most promising remedies are those that would increase leaders' incentives to use what is already available to them. Changing incentives in large organizations is never easy, but this study describes a promising way to do it. The result could be a significant redistribution of power in bureaucracies.

Herbert Kaufman is a senior fellow in Brookings Governmental Studies program. Michael Couzens, his assistant, is now studying law at the University of California (Berkeley).

ADMINISTRATIVE FEEDBACK

—

Monitoring Subordinates'
Behavior

HERBERT KAUFMAN
with the collaboration of
MICHAEL COUZENS

The Brookings Institution
WASHINGTON, D.C.

COPYRIGHT © 1973 BY
THE BROOKINGS INSTITUTION
1775 Massachusetts Avenue, N.W., Washington, D.C. 20036

Library of Congress Cataloging in Publication Data:
Kaufman, Herbert, 1922–
    Administrative feedback.

    Bibliography: p.
    1. United States—Executive departments—Management.
2. Communication in management.   3. Management
information systems.   I. Title.
JK421.K38   353   73-1085

ISBN 0-8157-4838-8
ISBN 0-8157-4837-x (pbk)

1 2 3 4 5 6 7 8 9

THE BROOKINGS INSTITUTION is an independent organization devoted to nonpartisan research, education, and publication in economics, government, foreign policy, and the social sciences generally. Its principal purposes are to aid in the development of sound public policies and to promote public understanding of issues of national importance.

The Institution was founded on December 8, 1927, to merge the activities of the Institute for Government Research, founded in 1916, the Institute of Economics, founded in 1922, and the Robert Brookings Graduate School of Economics and Government, founded in 1924.

The Board of Trustees is responsible for the general administration of the Institution, while the immediate direction of the policies, program, and staff is vested in the President, assisted by an advisory committee of the officers and staff. The by-laws of the Institution state, "It is the function of the Trustees to make possible the conduct of scientific research, and publication, under the most favorable conditions, and to safeguard the independence of the research staff in the pursuit of their studies and in the publication of the results of such studies. It is not a part of their function to determine, control, or influence the conduct of particular investigations or the conclusions reached."

The President bears final responsibility for the decision to publish a manuscript as a Brookings book or staff paper. In reaching his judgment on the competence, accuracy, and objectivity of each study, the President is advised by the director of the appropriate research program and weighs the views of a panel of expert outside readers who report to him in confidence on the quality of the work. Publication of a work signifies that it is deemed to be a competent treatment worthy of public consideration; such publication does not imply endorsement of conclusions or recommendations contained in the study.

The Institution maintains its position of neutrality on issues of public policy in order to safeguard the intellectual freedom of the staff. Hence interpretations or conclusions in Brookings publications should be understood to be solely those of the author or authors and should not be attributed to the Institution, to its trustees, officers, or other staff members, or to the organizations that support its research.

Foreword

I T   W O U L D   not be altogether surprising if the leaders of large public organizations occasionally wake up unnerved because they dream that employees at lower organizational levels do not do what the leaders want them to, or even what the leaders think they do. Most of the time, the leaders can doubtless reassure themselves that the fear is only a nightmare. "It couldn't actually happen," they could tell themselves; "I'd find out at once, in a dozen different ways."

But there must be times when the fear and the doubts will not be quieted. There has been recent evidence that disobedience occurs even in the military in wartime, the strength of hierarchy and discipline notwithstanding. How then can leaders be sure of what goes on in less disciplined organizations? "Do I really know about the behavior of my subordinates?" they must wonder once in a while.

If they look through the literature on organizations, they will find little empirical evidence on which to base an answer to that question. The study described in this book is an effort to add to that meager store.

Herbert Kaufman is Senior Fellow in the Brookings Governmental Studies program, and Michael Couzens was a research assistant in that program through the life of this study. In the course of their work, the greatest debt the authors incurred was to the officers and employees of the nine federal organizations examined in detail. There are far too many people to permit acknowledging each individual's assistance separately, but the extent of their help is a tribute to the openness of the bureaucracy.

At Brookings, drafts of the manuscript were reviewed by

Thomas E. Cronin, Leonard Goodwin, Morton H. Halperin, Phillip S. Hughes, Allen Schick, Leon V. Sigal, David T. Stanley, Gilbert Y. Steiner, and James L. Sundquist. Arnold Kanter and Francis E. Rourke were among the non-Brookings critics of the penultimate version; a third reader, who remains anonymous, also took pains with that draft. In editing the manuscript, Alice M. Carroll helped clarify the authors' thinking and smoothed their language. Radmila Reinhart provided secretarial assistance.

The views expressed in this study are the authors' and should not be attributed to the trustees, officers, or other staff members of the Brookings Institution.

KERMIT GORDON
President

January 1973
Washington, D.C.

Contents

ADMINISTRATIVE
FEEDBACK

Research Objective

ADMINISTRATORS and students of administration commonly assume that the leaders of organizations are informed about the activities of their subordinates. Both theory and practice rest on this premise.

It is not an unreasonable assumption. The ways in which leaders can learn about the administrative behavior of the people in the ranks below them are numerous and varied. Indeed, they get much information without deliberately seeking it, some of it against their will.

Suppose, however, the assumption were inaccurate in many respects—that leaders are ordinarily much more poorly informed about what their subordinates are doing than they and organization theorists think they are. We think the consequences of the misconception would be important both theoretically and practically.

In an effort to determine whether the assumption on the one hand or the doubt about it on the other is closer to the truth, we studied a number of federal bureaus. We confined the study to "administrative feedback," defined as all the processes by which the bureau leaders—the whole headquarters—are apprised of subordinate behavior down to the lowest organizational level. We did not examine "substantive feedback"—the flow of information advising headquarters how close the activities of the organizations come to the substantive targets set by the leaders— since it is possible for an organization to miss its targets badly for the very reason that subordinates faithfully comply with erroneous directives issued by their leaders. We concerned ourselves only with the question, Does it appear in these agencies that the information about subordinates reaching headquarters is sufficient for leaders to judge accurately whether their subordinates are complying with directives?

IMPORTANCE OF ADMINISTRATIVE FEEDBACK

Administrative feedback is a vital element in organizations because subordinate compliance does not automatically follow upon the issuance of orders and instructions by leaders. When managers die and go to heaven, they may find themselves in charge of organizations in which subordinates invariably, cheerfully, and fully do as they are bid. Not here on earth.

Tendencies toward Noncompliance by Subordinates

Halperin sums up the tendencies toward noncompliance in three categories: the subordinates don't know what their superiors want, they can't do what their superiors want, or they refuse to do what their superiors want.[1]

In any large organization, subordinates inevitably receive clashing and contradictory cues and signals from above. From the standpoint of the individual employee, an organization looks like a funnel with the employee at the throat of it; at each level above, various specialists issue instructions (frequently "in the name of" their chiefs) to be executed at the lowest level, and the higher the level of the initiators, the more numerous and finely specialized are the jurisdictions of the staff. Despite efforts to reconcile instructions, many directives come down without regard to those from other sources. When this happens, subordinates may have to decide for themselves what their situations require, picking and choosing among the directives for justification.

This obligation may be thrust on them by the inescapable ambiguities as well as the inconsistencies of the instructions to

1. Morton H. Halperin, "Bureaucratic Politics and Foreign Policy" (Brookings Institution, planned for publication in 1973), Chap. 15. See also Herbert Kaufman, *The Forest Ranger* (paperback ed., Johns Hopkins Press, 1967), Pt. 1.

them. Leaders have to draft directives in general terms designed to guide behavior in a wide variety of circumstances, and to permit sensible responses to unanticipated conditions. In any concrete situation, therefore, a subordinate may find that any one of several general statements is applicable, even if issued by only one person.

Furthermore, statutes and regulations stay on the books indefinitely. The accumulation comes to embody provisions of uncertain origin and intent with incompatible requirements as successive generations of leaders take over. From this corpus of material, it is not always clear what an employee is supposed to do in particular cases.

But even if a subordinate has no doubts about what his superiors would like him to do in a given situation, and even if he would sincerely like to do what he is told to do, he will occasionally find it *impossible* to comply. Sometimes it is because his work load prevents him from maintaining maximum standards of quality, as is the case when a small work force is spread thin. Sometimes it is because he has not had adequate training or experience. Sometimes it is because the state of the art he practices is not sufficiently advanced. Confronted by demands he cannot satisfy, he will fashion his own policies to handle the situation. His own policies often do not coincide with the policies of his leaders.

Of course, subordinates may know precisely what is expected of them, be perfectly capable of doing it, and still not do it. What they are asked to do may offend their personal principles or their interpretation of professional ethics or their extraorganizational loyalties and commitments or their self-interest. Leadership directives to end racial discrimination, for example, have been weakened or nullified in some areas by the inability or refusal of subordinates to transgress deeply ingrained prejudices. Attempts to transfer authority from functional officers to territorial officers have been known to fail because subordinates continue to acknowledge the authority of the former and to ignore the latter. Resistance by subordinates is not easy to detect when it takes place surreptitiously; open rebellion is much more visible. But people usually have to be pushed quite far before they resort to overt disobedience or strikes or revolution; more often, when orders from above conflict sharply with their values, they quietly construe the orders in a way that makes them tolerable. Organization policies may thus be amended at lower administrative levels.

Effects of Noncompliance by Subordinates

If what the leaders of organizations want is altered by subordinate action, their leadership is to that extent undermined; while total obedience can scarcely be expected, given the variability of human beings and the tendencies toward noncompliance, the limits and the frequency of deviation must be fairly narrow if the term *leadership* is to have much meaning. There are no leaders if there are no followers.

If leaders exert but little influence on the actions of subordinates, then one of the axioms of democratic government ceases to apply. In general terms, democracy in the modern state presupposes that changing a handful of officials in high places will ultimately change the actions of thousands of employees throughout the system. In fact, the short-ballot movement in the United States sprang from the inference that the actions of the employees could *more easily* be influenced by changing a small number of leaders than by electing large numbers of officials, the reasoning being that the diffusion of responsibility obscures visibility and accountability. To a greater or lesser extent, virtually all commentators on democracy in the same way take for granted the essential contribution of leadership. Subordinate compliance is thus a pillar of democratic government.

That organization theory and democratic philosophy would be shaken by subordinate noncompliance is a matter of concern mostly to intellectuals. That the effectiveness of the leaders of organizations, especially of democratic organizations, may in this way be reduced is probably a matter of more widespread concern.

Administrative Feedback and Compliance

We assume administrative feedback and subordinate compliance are closely linked. That is not to say fear of detection is the chief (let alone the sole) reason why subordinates comply with the wishes of their superiors. We believe the ability to elicit obedience depends not only on sanctions (both rewards and punishments) but on the employee's sense of legitimacy (the feeling he ought to obey), of identification (the feeling of loyalty to an organization and to his superiors), and of confidence (the feeling that another person knows more).[2] We do not, however, underestimate the utility of sanctions, positive and negative, when they are employed with subtlety. To employ sanctions effectively, leaders must know what their subordinates are doing, for they may reward and punish the wrong subordinates or the wrong behavior if they are inadequately informed, and may thus encourage disobedience instead of compliance. Sanctions therefore depend on feedback.

Leaders also need to be able to correct and redirect subordinate behavior when it starts to drift away from the patterns they desire. The major contribution of administrative feedback to administration is probably not its threat of exposure and of penalties and rewards; rather, it lies in the enhancement of leaders' capacities to neutralize tendencies toward noncompliance by enabling the leaders to clarify instructions, improve training, accommodate grants of authority and other resources to the requirements of the subordinates' jobs, and reshape incentives so subordinates are not impelled to depart from top-level pronouncements. All these measures imply leadership knowledge of subordinate behavior and of the reasons for failures to comply. Such knowledge, in turn, comes only from an adequate system of administrative feedback.

SEEMING IMPROBABILITY OF NONCOMPLIANCE

When we reflect on the number of ways organization leaders can acquire information about the activities of their subordinates, particularly in the federal government, we understand why administrative feedback has been so little studied. An abundance of

2. See Herbert A. Simon, Donald W. Smithburg, and Victor A. Thompson, *Public Administration* (Knopf, 1950), pp. 188–201.

feedback seems to be inevitable; indeed, it is often thrust upon leaders.

Planned Methods of Administrative Feedback

In every organization, even the most decentralized ones, at least some of the actions initiated by subordinates are prohibited from taking effect until specifically approved by a designated superior. Clearance procedures usually emphasize prevention rather than detection of deviation from higher level policy decisions. But they also force upon the attention of higher levels a good deal of information about operations at lower levels.

Inevitably, however, the great bulk of information about subordinate activity is compiled after actions have been completed, and usually consists of data provided by the very subordinates who took the actions. Most of the information is passed along through standard forms filled out routinely at lower levels and assembled and tabulated at higher levels. Sometimes, however, reporting is very personal and free in form, as in the debriefing of personnel returned from a journey and in narrative documents. Records and reporting systems vary widely from organization to organization, but it is probably safe to say there is no large organization without some kind of prescribed reporting practice.

At the same time, organizations rarely rely exclusively on reports for administrative feedback because of the temptations of those who describe their own activities to exaggerate achievements and to understate or conceal deficiencies. Reporting requirements and forms are often designed to maximize the probabilities that falsifications will be detected, but even these strategies are seldom sufficient to reassure leaders. That is why almost every organization relies on site visits to lower levels by representatives of higher levels. Presumably these disinterested firsthand observations keep reports more accurate than they would otherwise be and incidentally produce information and insights that no documentary sources could ever capture and convey.

When things go wrong in spite of efforts to prevent failures, a common organizational response is to launch a study, by agency personnel or consultants or both, to find the cause and fix the blame. Like inspections and audits, investigations and inquiries involve visits to work sites, but they are usually more intensive and searching than routine, periodic examinations. Consequently, when something happens that triggers an investigation, the investigation commonly turns up information on subordinate practices not related only to the immediate cause. This adds both to the store of management information about subordinate behavior and to subordinate incentives to avoid deficiencies that might provoke such inquiries.

From time to time, many organizations bring together their field and headquarters personnel in face-to-face gatherings (or employ conference telephone circuits for comparable purposes). These gatherings serve a variety of ends, both substantive and symbolic, of which administrative feedback is only one. Nevertheless, they afford opportunities for leaders to examine people who have personal knowledge of, and varied perspectives on, conditions and operations in the field. Events and problems that escape other data-gathering methods may occasionally get caught in this net.

The information collected by all the foregoing methods flows on the initiative of the higher levels calling up data from below. Some methods permit personnel at the *lower* levels to take the initiative; machinery for the presentation and resolution of employee grievances is of this nature. Of course, it serves more to apprise leaders of what is being done *to* subordinates than what is being done *by* them, but some of the complaints doubtless indicate obliquely what the realities of life at the lower levels are.

Similarly, suggestion boxes used by some organizations facilitate communication of ideas and complaints from lower administrative levels to higher authorities, and presumably thereby provide at least some marginal clues to the state of affairs in the lower organizational reaches.

Other devices facilitate administrative feedback from customers and clients unhappy with the way they have been dealt with by organization members. The complaint bureau in department stores is probably the most familiar of these, though perhaps rivaled in familiarity by the telephone companies' "service representatives." In government, the treatment of complaints is not often assigned to a separate unit in this fashion, but recent experiments with such an office, adapted from the Scandinavian ombudsman, may constitute vanguards of a modest trend in that direction.

More common in public agencies is an established procedure whereby the clients of the agencies can appeal from decisions and actions of lower level personnel, the chain of appeal running through the administrative hierarchy and ultimately to the courts. Like complaint-handling units, they are channels only for expressions of discontent, and not all subordinate noncompliance produces discontent, so the information they yield has an intrinsic bias. For information about clientele dissatisfaction, however, they serve as a good barometer.

Before public agencies can promulgate some kinds of rules or decisions, they are required by statute to hold public hearings, of which they must give ample notice to all parties likely to be affected by the actions. The ostensible reason is that factors that might otherwise not enter into agencies' decisions will have a fair chance of being impressed on the decision-making process. On the whole, these are occasions when people elaborate their interests rather than describe and analyze subordinate activity. But hearings do give clients and their representatives some chances to ventilate discontents sparked by encounters with subordinates, and these chances are sometimes seized.

Another way clients and customers are afforded opportunities to present their views to organization leaders—usually in the field of business—is through opinion polls. The crudest form is the distribution of cards asking the subjects to check items about the quality of service they received, but some firms use sophisticated sampling techniques, questionnaires, and personal interviews.

Fortuitous Administrative Feedback
Even if an organization were to employ none of the planned

8

methods of feedback, its leaders would still receive a flow of information about subordinate behavior through processes and channels *not* of their own devising. Not so much by chance as by the characteristics of the world we live in, information is virtually thrust upon them whether they will it or not.

For example, some people do not use the procedures established by organizations for the handling of complaints even when the procedures are simple and readily available—perhaps because they have little confidence that they will get satisfaction if they appeal to one part of a bureaucracy for aid against another, perhaps because they are confused or intimidated by large organizations. Instead, they write directly to the organization chief. In practice, few chiefs are likely to see such mail personally. But they do have within their reach, if they care to take advantage of it, an index of some qualities of subordinate behavior.

Even more important are the "intercessor groups" that choose or are obliged to take the responsibility of representing clienteles and customers, both collectively and individually, in administrative proceedings, in and before legislative bodies, or in suits brought in the courts.[3] The most familiar form is the interest group (or "pressure group"), usually consisting of, and financed by, a portion of the population for which it claims to speak; veterans' organizations, business associations, labor unions, farmers' groups, and, more recently, consumer associations and welfare rights organizations are examples. But they appear in many other forms as well: some newspapers and radio and television stations, for instance, have offered their services as intermediaries to assist people frustrated in their efforts to get justice from public and private organizations. Public-interest law firms have sprung up to perform this service. Some community or civic groups—for example, the American Civil Liberties Union—furnish the same sort of assistance. Sometimes one administrative agency (such as an equal opportunities commission or a civil rights body) will go to the aid of a complainant before another agency. Political parties

3. See Gilbert Y. Steiner, *The State of Welfare* (Brookings Institution, 1971), pp. 321–25.

traditionally rendered this sort of help, and though it looks as if they are losing this function to other institutions, they are still active in this way in many localities. And, of course, legislators routinely take up with administrative officers the causes of their constituents, and legislative committees may be inspired by some constituent outcries to conduct investigations of the conditions giving rise to the distress.

All of the preceding kinds of unplanned feedback originate in clientele or customer objections to agency actions or decisions. Some feedback, however, comes from the normal interactions of organizations with each other. In the ordinary course of events, for example, staff agencies, such as budget, personnel, administrative management, audit, legal counsel, and public relations can be expected to turn up some information for line executives about the behavior of line subordinates. Agencies with overlapping assignments may do the same; environmental protection units, for instance, may call attention to facets of the work of highway bureaus or economic development departments that might otherwise escape notice. Similarly, competitive agencies may reveal a good deal about each other's field activities, as a park service and a forestry agency and a mineral resources bureau might. Legislative committees charged with taxation or appropriations or oversight of administration may focus attention on patterns of action at lower administrative levels. The complexity of large-scale organizations makes for innumerable interfaces with other organizations, with the result that data about subordinate activities flow in from many sources even if no one has requested them.

Some individuals and organizations thrive on exposing shortcomings in public agencies, employing sensational publicity to influence policy or simply to increase their own visibility. Reporters from the mass media, public prosecutors, grand juries, civic groups, and public investigatory commissions illustrate the point. To be sure, they do not concentrate their fire exclusively on field personnel, high-level decisions usually absorbing most of their attention. But they frequently enliven their stories with anecdotes about field behavior and sometimes make field behavior the center of their concerns. Agency headquarters alerted to noncompliant subordinate activity by exposés seldom welcome the discovery and doubtless wish they would get less unplanned feedback of this kind. It keeps coming anyway.

Subordinates themselves give fortuitous clues about their own activities to higher organizational levels when they seek clarification of policy pronouncements and other orders from above. Every time subordinates seek advice from their superiors about conflicts in orders or their applicability to specific cases, they add a little to the information available to superiors about conditions at the lower levels. In effect, they establish a process of informal, voluntary clearance.

Information also filters back to headquarters in an informal way by word of mouth. Overlapping circles of acquaintances, membership in clubs and community groups and political parties and churches and professional associations, and casual comments and observations by people recently back from trips to the field can furnish hints about events at lower levels. Amid all the gossip and rumor are found kernels of fact from which a great deal can be learned about the work of subordinates. Without their lifting a finger to obtain it, leaders find such information often drifts into their range of hearing.

Multiple Channels of Feedback

Through the administrative structure, through Congress, and through the courts, intelligence about the administrative behavior of subordinates streams into bureau headquarters. Through the mass media, nongovernmental groups of all kinds, and the parties, data are pumped in. Isn't it obvious that administrative feedback must be plentiful? Does it make any sense to inquire into the obvious?

DOUBTS ABOUT COMPLIANCE

In spite of the abundance of ways in which administrative feedback theoretically can reach the upper levels of organizations, bits of evidence surface now and then suggesting things are *not* going at lower levels as leaders apparently think they are. For example, Harold Wilensky contends that

> where field or branch products and local operating conditions vary, surveillance machinery proliferates. Such machinery is often ineffectual. . . . Where the social and doctrinal distance between inspectors and local operators is great, the resulting information blockage may imperil top leaders' awareness of and accommodation to local problems.[4]

One of the most dramatic illustrations is a mid-1960s scandal in which a large number of reputable firms lent money to a shady businessman against collateral in the form of stored oil only to find out, at a cost of millions of dollars, that the oil was not actually there and that their inspectors had failed to check the storage tanks properly.[5] In the same period a Texas businessman obtained loans secured by tanks of fertilizer that subsequently turned out to be wholly fictitious; nobody conducted an examination prior to the transaction to determine whether the security was as claimed.[6] More recently a multimillion-dollar robbery of an exclusive New York hotel succeeded at least in part because the hotel staff failed to close the vault as required by the management.[7]

Less spectacular, but no less relevant, was a disclosure in Newark that night guards hired and paid by the Board of Education never appeared at the locations they were to protect.[8] In New York, many policemen on night duty were found to spend much of their

4. Harold L. Wilensky, *Organizational Intelligence: Knowledge and Policy in Government and Industry* (Basic Books, 1967), pp. 60–61.

5. Ibid., pp. 88–93.

6. Billy Sol Estes was convicted of fraud in a Texas court as a result. Subsequently, he petitioned for a retrial in federal district court, contending that a witness, who denied knowing that the fertilizer tanks did not exist when he (the witness) had accepted them as security for a mortgage, had testified falsely. According to Estes, the fictitiousness of the tanks was known. The court did not believe this contention, however, and denied the petition. Meanwhile, subcommittees in both the Senate and the House of Representatives criticized inspection procedures in the Department of Agriculture that made such offenses possible. See *New York Times*, Jan. 25, 1963; Oct. 1 and 12, 1964; April 12 and 23, 1966.

7. Eric Pace, *New York Times*, Jan. 4, 1972.

8. Joseph Sullivan, *New York Times*, Dec. 16, 1971.

time sleeping instead of cruising.[9] In many cities, appraisers responsible for setting the value of houses against which federal guarantees of loans were provided did not visit the sites and inspect the properties, with the result that the low-income beneficiaries were assisted in taking over run-down, over-valued structures that they could not maintain, and the government ultimately found itself holding hundreds of these deserted, dilapidated buildings.[10] In a county near Washington, more than a dozen swimming pools denied health permits and ordered not to open were found to be in operation after people fell ill at one of them, and many more were found to be operating without even having applied for the permit required by law.[11] In a national survey, private physicians admitted that they reported only one venereal disease case out of nine to public health authorities.[12] According to a study of a maximum security prison in New Jersey,

the guard is frequently reluctant to enforce the full range of the institution's regulations. The guard frequently fails to report infractions of the rules which have occurred before his eyes. The guard often transmits forbidden information to inmates, such as plans for searching particular cells in a surprise raid for contraband. The guard often neglects elementary security requirements.[13]

A former assistant secretary of state, reflecting on his experience in government, observed, "When a man moves to the second level of coordination, at which he attempts to bring together a number of agencies to deal with common problems . . . he cannot quite be sure just what the agencies involved are really doing."[14] He admitted that when his office estimated certain government-wide expenditures, it used "a combination of fact, guesswork and semantic ingenuity," and he explained, "It is just the fact that the

9. David Burnham, *New York Times*, Dec. 16, 17, 18, and 21, 1968.

10. Don Ball, "Foreclosures Costing FHA Millions," *Washington Post*, Dec. 12, 1971, p. G1.

11. Herbert H. Denton, *Washington Post*, June 9, 1971.

12. Jane E. Brody, *New York Times*, March 17, 1970.

13. Gresham A. Sykes, *The Society of Captives: A Study of a Maximum Security Prison* (Princeton University Press, 1958), p. 54; see also, pp. 53–58.

14. Charles Frankel, *High on Foggy Bottom* (Harper & Row, 1969), p. 182.

government doesn't know what it is doing."[15] Similarly, an official study of a mass killing of Vietnamese civilians by American troops disclosed that at each successive higher level in the military hierarchy the reported number of victims was reduced, so that the highest levels had no idea of the extent of the tragedy despite two separate command channels for the transmission of news about events in the field. A field commander subsequently declared that every large combat unit has similar episodes "hidden somewhere."[16] Comparable distortions occurred in the Postal Service, where officials for a time believed new goals for prompt service were being met; in fact, performance was much worse than they thought because postal workers detected test letters sent out by the superiors and gave those letters special treatment. "We were," said one official, "lured into a false sense of security . . . by the people in the field."[17] All of which confirms the opinion of an academic observer of organizations that "upward communication . . . is at least as inadequate as downward communication and probably less accurate because of the selective filtering of information which subordinates feed to their superiors."[18]

The practices cited in some of these examples had been going on for years before coming to light. Some doubtless still do.

The question naturally arises, How is it possible for the apparently deficient behavior of some subordinates to have escaped detection for so long if the abundance of modes of administrative feedback allegedly makes it impossible for such deficiencies to go unnoticed for prolonged periods? Is it not possible that feedback systems do *not* work as they are believed to? That the planned methods of feedback, for instance, are manipulated to withhold information subordinates consider detrimental to their interests? That fewer people take the trouble to press their complaints than

15. Ibid., p. 181.

16. William Beecher, *New York Times*, March 18, 19, and 27, 1970; May 25, 1971.

17. Robert J. Samuelson, "Why the Mail Is a Mess," *Washington Post*, Nov. 26, 1972, p. B4.

18. Rensis Likert, *New Patterns of Management* (McGraw-Hill, 1961), p. 47.

is commonly alleged? That journalists and scholars pay scant attention to subordinate behavior and concentrate their attention instead on high policy? That for these and a score of similar reasons, leaders are not alerted to all the facets of activities at lower levels that they think are automatically called to their attention? The leader of a public organization who is aware of the inventory of possible feedback modes might quite understandably dismiss this danger. But that very confidence may blind him to the gravity of the risk. Our research objective was to find out if his confidence was justified.

But here we were confronted by a paradox. The instances adduced to question the confidence in administrative feedback might just as logically be advanced to confirm that confidence. After all, they are available as evidence for the very reason that they were exposed by feedback. In fact, if we ourselves turned up examples of subordinate noncompliance in our research, they would show that this form of feedback, as one among the long list, does indeed function successfully. Instead of raising specters, the revelations could be interpreted to lay them to rest.

We were not satisfied with this interpretation, for it seemed unlikely the difficulties could have proceeded to the extreme stage they reached before detection if the administrative feedback systems in the organizations affected had been working as the inventory of feedback modes implies they should. Moreover, the persistence of the difficulties for as long as they lasted inclined us to wonder if there were not others that had gone on much longer, perhaps never to be reported. How could we know we were not seeing the small tip of the proverbial iceberg? This was the question we set out to answer.

❧ II ❧

Research Strategy

IDEALLY, the way to study administrative feedback would be to examine all the information about subordinate behavior that flows into the headquarters of a great variety of organizations, to analyze the transformation of the information that takes place in the collection, processing, and transmission of the raw data, and to appraise the fit between the data in all stages of all the pipelines on the one hand and the actual behavior of subordinate personnel on the other. What organization leaders think is going on ought to be compared with (a) what their administrative feedback tells them is going on and (b) what is actually going on. Analysis of the content of the feedback, the use made of it, and its impact on behavior at all administrative levels ought also to be included in an exhaustive investigation.

Obviously, such a task would require an army of researchers, massive resources, and years of inquiry. Because little attention has been given to administrative feedback,[1] we felt a cautious initial effort would be more appropriate. So we set ourselves a more modest objective: to examine feedback practices and experience in a small number of organizations without aspiring to exhaustiveness or to methodological rigor. We discovered very early we would have to rely heavily on impressionistic and anecdotal evidence, and that the results would be inconclusive. But we thought impressions based on empirical studies would be more enlightening than the surmise and speculation that now surround the subject.

1. See Bibliographical Note, pp. 81–83, below.

THE SPECIMEN ORGANIZATIONS

We decided all our "specimens" would be bureaus of the federal government in Washington, where administrative feedback ought to be particularly well developed because of the requirements of accountability and control in a democratic polity and because records and officials are comparatively open. Furthermore, most bureaus are large enough to exhibit the characteristics of all large organizations, yet small enough to permit fairly thorough study in a relatively short time. Although no two bureaus are exactly alike, they share enough attributes to allow comparisons, and their differences assure a wide range of practices.

We thought it likely that the character of a bureau's operations would affect the major features of its administrative feedback system. We consequently tried to include among our specimens both bureaus that directly administer programs and bureaus engaged primarily in disbursing money to other governmental jurisdictions that actually do the work, and both regulatory bureaus (engaged in establishing and policing standards of products and performance by citizens and firms) and service bureaus (doing things to help or improve their clienteles). In the case of intergovernmental programs, we opted to treat the recipients of bureau-administered funds as though they were subordinates of the administering agencies in order to sharpen the comparisons and contrasts between feedback practices in direct and intergovernmental administration, and we found this artificial convention useful even though it exaggerated some seeming shortcomings in some of the bureaus. Moreover, many bureaus combine regulatory and service responsibilities, and anyway, what is a regulatory activity to one person may constitute a service to another. Despite these problems, the classification doubtless broadened the range of organizational types in our sample.

We had hoped to distribute our specimens equally among the four categories. Declinations to take part in the study and reorganizations during our inquiries confined our examination to programs in nine bureaus, as follows:

17

Regulatory bureaus administering their own programs:
  Federal Aviation Administration (flight safety program only)
  Food and Drug Administration (administration of food
    standards only)
  Bureau of Mines (coal mine safety program only)
Regulatory bureaus administering intergovernmental
programs:
  Law Enforcement Assistance Administration
Service bureaus administering their own programs:
  Bureau of Prisons
  Bureau of Indian Affairs
  National Ocean Survey
Service bureaus administering intergovernmental programs:
  Forest Service (state and private forestry only)
  Bureau of Elementary and Secondary Education (aid to
    school districts with heavy concentrations of
    "disadvantaged children" only).

This selection gave us two bureaus or programs each in the Departments of Justice (Prisons, Law Enforcement Assistance), Health, Education, and Welfare (Food and Drug, Education), and Interior (Mines, Indian Affairs); and one each in the Departments of Transportation (Aviation), Agriculture (Forest), and Commerce (Ocean). Yet the sample was by no means "representative" of the whole executive branch of the federal government; indeed, it is doubtful that any sample *can* be typical because the diversity of federal responsibilities and the degree of specialization are so great. Conspicuously absent were the independent regulatory commissions and the other federal agencies not lodged in executive departments, agencies in international relations and defense, and agencies that work largely by letting contracts to private interests. Still, the specimens constituted an interesting and varied collection, and we were confident they could tell us a great deal about administrative feedback.

THUMBNAIL PROFILES

Regulatory agencies review the behavior of specified citizens and firms to ensure their observance of externally imposed requirements. All three of the regulatory bureaus with directly administered programs conduct their operations through inspectors who live and work in all parts of the far-flung agency jurisdictions.[2] In the Federal Aviation Administration, where we focused on the safety programs administered by the Flight Standards Service, the inspectors check on the construction, operation, and maintenance of commercial and private aircraft and their navigational equipment, and also on the qualifications and performance of aircraft pilots, engineers, mechanics, air taxi services, repair stations, and so forth. In the Food and Drug Administration there is an inspectorate whose duties include checking on the composition and safety of foods in interstate commerce, backed by field laboratories that conduct tests and perform chemical analyses. In the Bureau of Mines, coal mine inspectors examine between two thousand and three thousand mines for structural safety, for adequacy of ventilation, for conditions that can produce explosions, for proper types and handling of equipment and explosives, and for hazardous practices by miners and mine operators generally. All three bureaus concentrate on deterring violations of announced standards by detecting transgressions, obtaining corrections when possible, and proceeding against offenders when necessary.

Service activities, on the other hand, are directed toward helping people and firms get on with their own lives and activities in socially constructive ways. Though elements of both regulation and service can be found in most agencies, there is a distinct difference in emphasis. Thus, the National Ocean Survey helps everyone engaged in navigation by producing nautical and aeronautical charts, predicting tides and currents, conducting marine and geo-

2. Sketches of the nine bureaus are based on the *United States Government Organization Manual* and annual reports of the individual bureaus or their parent agencies. In some cases, additional details were supplied by the agencies.

detic and oceanographic surveys, and monitoring the earth's geophysical fields and seismic activities. The Bureau of Indian Affairs provides a whole range of services for the 450,000 residents of 200 Indian reservations, including welfare, education, training, guidance, financial assistance, technical assistance, and industrial development assistance, all with the aim of helping the clients achieve economic "self-sufficiency," full participation in American life, and "equal citizenship privileges and responsibilities." Even the Bureau of Prisons, which may not seem on the surface to be a service bureau, includes in its program the provision of training, advice, education, medical (including psychiatric) assistance, and other services to encourage and help a population of about 20,000 inmates in twenty-nine federal correctional institutions make a satisfactory and socially acceptable adjustment to life on the outside when they are released.

In still another position are the bureaus administering intergovernmental programs, for they must rely on the personnel not only of other federal agencies but of state or local government agencies to conduct the actual operations that accomplish program objectives. It is not strictly accurate to treat such personnel as subordinates of the federal bureaus that support them; we have nevertheless done so to highlight the special feedback problems of this method of administration.

The smallest of the intergovernmental service programs was the Forest Service's long-established aid to state public forestry agencies for their own development and for aid to private owners of forest lands and woodlots. In fiscal year 1971, some $24 million was distributed to the fifty state foresters for these purposes. By contrast, approximately $1.4 billion was distributed by the Bureau of Elementary and Secondary Education (a unit in the U.S. Office of Education) to some 16,000 local school districts serving dense concentrations of poor families in order to improve the quality of the schooling received by children in those districts.

The only intergovernmental program administered by a regulatory agency in our sample—the Law Enforcement Assistance Administration (LEAA)—worked largely through the states in the same way as the Forest Service. In fiscal year 1971 it furnished outlays of almost $400 million, most of it going to a designated state office in each state, to assist state and local governments in achieving a wide range of improvements in law enforcement and administration of criminal justice. A portion of the funds to the states was required by law to pass through to localities; in addition, some discretionary funds were disbursed by the LEAA directly to local authorities.

SUBORDINATE DISCRETION IN THE NINE BUREAUS

At the lowest administrative levels in all these bureaus and pro-grams, the discretion vested in the personnel with whom the clients come in contact can be extremely important. Inspectors, for example, might be more lenient with some of the people and firms they regulate, more severe with others, thus according competitive advantages to one group over the other. Even if the inspectors are nondiscriminatory, they can devitalize regulation if they are unduly lenient, or if they are consistently inefficient in the detec-tion of violations of standards. By the same token, excessive zeal on the part of inspectors can impede the growth of enterprises performing valuable services or producing needed goods.

Similarly, there is some evidence that custodial officers com-monly do not subscribe to rehabilitation and service as practical goals in penal institutions, with the result that some are inclined to employ stern demonstrations of force to keep inmates in line, others give up hope and enter into arrangements with self-selected inmate leaders as a way of assuring their own safety and preserving order without great exertion, and still others may even sell privi-leges or assist prisoners in illegal activities for their own enrich-ment.

In the same way, the men and women on the ships, planes, and field parties collecting data for geophysical and navigational pur-poses could be meticulous and conscientious to a fault as they perform their functions in distant places, or they might take things a little easy when out on their own, perhaps estimating instead of taking the prescribed number of precise measurements when that makes their job simpler.

And so it goes also with the widely dispersed field activities on behalf of the American Indians, which may be performed in a paternalistic and authoritarian fashion or a permissive or indifferent one, and with all the intergovernmental programs, where the state and local officials and employees who receive federal funds may use them as their federal benefactors hope or, by subtle differences in emphasis and detail, modify substantially the impacts of the programs.

CHARACTER OF THE DATA

The importance of discretion in our specimen agencies intensified our doubts about the presumed efficiency of the feedback system. True, in view of the diverse modes and channels of administrative feedback in governmental organizations and the profound impact of the work of the nine bureaus on the lives and fortunes of so many people, the chances that the behavior of subordinates could depart very far or long from the intentions of bureau leaders without detection continued to seem remote. On the other hand, we did not consider it self-evident that there could really be enough feedback to let busy officials in Washington know what an inspector in an airplane factory in Seattle or Wichita does day by day, or how thorough an inspector of a Pennsylvania coal mine has been, or how exacting an inspector of a food-processing plant in California was. How could bureau leaders be fully informed about whether a prison guard in Georgia was stricter or more tolerant, let alone more untrustworthy, than the leaders would regard as compatible with proper operation of a correctional institution? How could they tell whether money intended to improve the education of children in a Dallas slum was spent in effective pursuit of that goal?

In order to find out, we studied the actual flow of data about subordinate behavior into the headquarters of the nine bureaus for over a year in 1970 and 1971. The materials were so varied in content and format, and the practices of each bureau so uniquely adapted to its objectives, that we elected to rely largely on impressions formed by brief but intensive immersion in the feedback procedures in each bureau. We perused reports of all kinds—routine, periodic, internal reports; reports of inspections and investigations; management surveys; audits, both internal and external; and academic and journalistic studies and commentaries in the bureaus' files. We read mail from the public, congressional mail, hearings, dockets, press files, and every other documentary source we could find. We interviewed line and staff members of headquarters staffs and, in a few instances, field personnel and interest-group spokesmen, seeking facts about feedback, opinions about it, attitudes toward it. As the information we assembled began to form patterns, the answer to our question began to emerge.

≫ III ≪

Administrative Feedback in the Specimen Agencies

A GREAT DEAL of information about subordinate behavior does indeed get back to headquarters. In two of the bureaus we studied, it is true, the information was much thinner than in the other seven, but both are agencies that operate intergovernmentally rather than directly in the field, and both programs are fairly new. In all the others there is such a flow of data that leaders who put all the data together and analyze them carefully may reasonably assume no important, persistent patterns of action at even the lowest administrative levels have escaped their notice.

Of course, putting the data together and analyzing them are not simple tasks. To say the raw material is available is therefore not the same as saying the finished product emerges from the processing. It is not the same as saying the leaders actually know everything going on below them (although many are clearly well informed about some particulars at any given moment). And it is not the same as saying subordinates are unquestionably compliant. It means only that in seven of the nine cases, leaders are at least in a position to figure out from the information furnished them by the various current modes of feedback whether their subordinates are largely in conformity with or in violation of the leaders' wishes and intentions.

FIVE MAJOR SOURCES

Five sources provided almost all the information reaching headquarters about subordinate behavior: reports, inspections, the "grapevine," investigations, and centralized administrative services. These alone are enough to keep seven of our nine bureaus amply supplied with data on compliance.

A Trail of Paper

Reporting turned out to be the heart of the feedback process, as orthodox administrative doctrine asserts. The trail of reports left behind by each field officer, particularly in the directly administered regulatory bureaus, is an ineradicable track. The track is especially prominent in the regulatory bureaus because field officers are often called to account for their actions in detail when their decisions are appealed or when litigation must be instituted by the government to enforce bureau decisions; the specific timing of correspondence and conversations, for example, can assume great significance in such cases. Moreover, inspectors are out in the field away from their immediate supervisors a good deal of the time. Partly for this reason, the regulatory bureaus require full statements of their activities.

The Flight Standards Service, for example, was responsible for more than 400 categories of recurring reports as of July 1970. Of these, over 350 were initiated within the Federal Aviation Administration (FAA), over 50 more were records and reports required from the public, and 3 were required by other government agencies or external sources. Over a quarter (98) of the 350 were monthly or more frequent (including 25 daily), another quarter (96) were quarterly or semiannual, and the remainder were annual or as specific events occurred. Many intersected the reports prepared by other components of the FAA, such as the near midair collision reports of the Air Traffic Service, the fiscal and accounting reports of the Office of Management Systems and the Office of Budget, and the legal enforcement reports of the Office of General Counsel. The opportunities for outside cross checks were thus plentiful. Even without them, however, the abundance of Flight Standards reports would have provided numerous internal verifications and insights.

But the directly administered service bureaus likewise receive numerous reports from their lower level personnel. The National

Ocean Survey, for instance, gets its data for charts partly from its ships and planes. Most of the data are electronically or photographically recorded. If the vehicles fail to cover their assigned terrain, it is at once evident to headquarters officials who assemble and interpret the data and construct charts from them. Headquarters staff can tell a great deal about what has been happening in the field merely by reviewing these records, by studying the data (including monthly accomplishment reports in which every unit of work done is entered) gathered for the Survey's forty-seven reports to the National Oceanic and Atmospheric Administration, and by comparing those data with trends perceptible in past records. Similarly, the Bureau of Prisons accumulates voluminous files on every prisoner in its custody, of which parts and summaries, sometimes running to hundreds of pages, are kept in Washington. These in turn can be compared with at least 130 statistical reports on every aspect of agency and institutional management. The two perspectives combined can alert the Washington staff to the quality of work in the field and the circumstances of the prisoners. In the Bureau of Indian Affairs, actions are recorded on more than 400 forms and communicated to managers in more than 400 different required reports (of which more than 140 are rendered monthly or more frequently and over 40 more are quarterly).

In the intergovernmental programs there is a divergence between the long-established state and private forestry program of the Forest Service and the newer programs of law enforcement assistance and aid to poverty-impacted school systems. The first is well developed, the last two not so advanced. The Forest Service, for example, at the time of our study, had just finished testing and was in process of installing a new procedure for reporting on assistance to private woodland owners and timber processors by state or federal forest officers; daily forms, with easily checked off details on each assist, will furnish information to be keypunched on cards once a week and sent to Washington for processing, tabular summary, and distribution to the states and to relevant officials in the U.S. Forest Service. Thus, the Washington office of the Forest Service will know almost as quickly as the state forestry agencies what the state field personnel are doing in connection with federally aided programs, and will know the *aggregate* results even *sooner*. Since the data can be assembled by functions, by territories, by organizational units, and by other categories, the information about activities in the field will be extraordinarily complete. Supplementing recurring fiscal reports, these accomplishment records provide rich, corroborating detail. The Law Enforcement Assistance Administration and the Bureau of Elementary and Secondary Education—partly because of the way their missions are defined, and partly, it seems, because they are still in the process of adjusting to massive responsibilities thrust quickly upon them—do not receive comparable accomplishment reports. For the same reasons, reports on the specific uses of federal funds in the localities are less frequent and fine spun; though the regional offices of LEAA, for instance, submit weekly free-form reports to headquarters, they depend for their impressions on quarterly narrative and fiscal reports from the states and on informal contacts rather than on systematic personal observation of lower governmental and administrative units within the states. In these two agencies, reporting to headquarters on what goes on at the lowest levels is much less elaborate than in the other seven.

Even in those bureaus and programs in which reporting practices are highly elaborated, not all reports illuminate subordinate behavior and some cast no light on it at all. This is hardly astonishing in view of the fact that the aim of some reporting requirements is not primarily to serve the ends of management, but to assure an influential congressman that his demands are satisfied, or to demonstrate to a staff agency that its injunctions are being observed, or to convince an interest group that its interests are not neglected. Such reporting requirements will often be resented and ridiculed, and therefore reduced in effectiveness.

Yet even reporting requirements that annoy bureau leaders can generate information about subordinate behavior. Specialized personnel and budgeting and other staff offices established within the bureaus to handle the procedures imposed from above typically become extremely knowledgeable about what goes on below. Wanted or not, the reports and records and intelligence to which these burdens give rise become part of the trail of paper informing the high command. Routine data on allocation of time, expenditure of money, travel, communication, supplies, and work load can be checked with reports on output. The claims of line officers can be compared with material gathered by, or collected in response to, staff units. Experienced superiors ought to have little difficulty detecting discrepancies and surmising from them what has actually been happening. The reports interlock. And the rapid spread of electronic data processing throughout the government multiplies the information that can be extracted from them by cross references and cross tabulations. Prominent as reporting already is among the modes of feedback, it is likely to grow even more important in consequence of the expanding use and capacity of computers.

Personal Inspection

Reports can be organized and presented to emphasize what the reporting officer wants stressed and to mute what he would rather conceal. Records can be manipulated. Critical events and physical structures do not disclose information unless they incite first-hand examinations that develop the facts. The trail of paper is apt to lead nowhere if it is not backed up by a system of personal inspections.[1]

But inspections do more than buttress other forms of feedback. If there were no other forms, bureau leaders could *still* learn a good deal about subordinate behavior by this means. In and of itself, it is a major source of information.

We are also persuaded that it is an excellent indicator of the state of the whole feedback system in a bureau. Although it is the mode we would recommend for an agency that could use only

1. In this section, "inspection" refers to personal review of subordinate administrative levels by representatives of higher headquarters, not to surveys of clients by line employees (such as safety inspectors).

one feedback technique, we have the impression that any agency that *does* take pains to set and maintain a carefully designed inspection procedure is usually strong in all other modes of feedback as well. Perhaps this obtains because it is comparatively easy to set up the other modes, and one can have greater confidence in them if they are reinforced by inspectors than is likely without inspections. At any rate, bureaus with good inspection systems seem usually to have good feedback generally. Not all inspections of subordinate operations are conducted by the bureaus themselves. When higher headquarters look into the bureaus, they sometimes visit field installations also. It is the internal inspections, however, that normally produce the bulk of the information about lower levels.

Inspection practices varied widely among and within the specimen bureaus. The Forest Service has a chief inspector whose job it is to plan and organize "general integrating inspections" (total evaluations of all dimensions of management and of substantive performance) throughout the agency, although the teams that actually conduct the inspections are regular members of the line and staff components of the Service rather than a separate and distinct corps. The teams survey physical conditions and interview scores of people in the communities they visit as well as state officials and their own field personnel. These searching probes reach every major subdivision of the Service, including the multi-state areas through which the state and private forestry program is administered, at least once every few years, and they sample the lesser subdivisions as well. They are both broad and deep.

In addition, and more frequently, teams specializing in individual functions (fire control, timber management, wildlife management, for example) visit every state receiving federal fiscal assistance to see how the federal money is spent and how well the function is performed generally. There are also separate fiscal audits of the books of the state forestry agencies.

The findings and recommendations of all inspection teams are discussed with the people inspected before they are written up, the emphasis in the Forest Service being on training rather than exposure. The written reports are extensive and detailed, and rich in information about what happens in the field. Especially interesting is the fact that the state foresters seem to welcome these inquiries even though federal funds constitute only a small part of state expenditures on the assisted programs; apparently, the inspectors are regarded as consultants rather than policemen, as helpers rather than informers, as friends rather than adversaries. The result is an abundance of data in Forest Service headquarters about how things are going in the states.

The Flight Standards Service (FSS) in the Federal Aviation Administration has an office similar to that of the chief inspector of the Forest Service, and uses it in much the same way. The Evaluation Unit attached to the Office of the Director of the FSS mobilizes specialists from all parts of headquarters to conduct reviews of operations in regional and district offices on a regular basis, surveying technical, administrative, and fiscal practices. In addition, the Evaluation Unit has available to it the findings of the Systemwide Analysis Program (SWAP), run out of the regional offices. SWAP teams, often comprising numbers of regional officers expert in every phase of field responsibilities, usually accompanied by some Washington office people, descend unannounced on district offices and inspect all aspects of their functioning; these are management, technical, and financial audits seldom surpassed for thoroughness, and the voluminous reports on them are passed along to central headquarters. As in the Forest Service, the emphasis is on the correction of error rather than on the apprehension of wrongdoers. As in the Forest Service, the outcome is extensive information about field behavior flowing to the top level of the bureau.

On the other hand, regular inspection forces and procedures for supervising use of funds under Title I of the Elementary and Secondary Education Act, the legislation providing aid to school districts with large numbers of poor children, were just being organized in the Bureau of Elementary and Secondary Education at the time of our study. The bureau had always regarded its legislative mandate as the automatic disbursement of funds allocated by formula rather than as the monitoring and policing of the recipients—an attitude formed in the long controversy over federal "control" of education—so the policy is not surprising.[2] The collective political influence of the recipients, the state and local public education officials composing the bureau's constituency, could exceed the power of the bureau in any head-on clash; the bureau was not eager for the kind of battles that might emerge from inspections of the recipients' actual use of the federal grants. So not until there were widely publicized charges from other quarters that the money was often improperly spent did the bureau begin to gear itself for intensive on-the-ground checks.

In the Law Enforcement Assistance Administration, where care is taken not to violate the principle that law enforcement is a state and local function, emphasis has been placed on encouraging and helping the *state* authorities to keep track and control of 30,000 subgrants at the lower levels; federal officials do not themselves conduct field inspections for this purpose (although regional officers sometimes accompany state inspectors visiting local grantees and pass observations back to Washington in regular reports). The increasingly frequent and thorough federal audits necessarily concentrate on documentation rather than on personal observations by the auditors. Feedback to LEAA headquarters from on-the-ground surveillance is thus largely indirect and limited.

The remaining five agencies range between these limiting cases, though they tend to cluster on the higher end of the scale (that is, toward stronger rather than weaker inspection practices). Their procedures are not as fully scheduled or spelled out as the Forest Service's or Flight Standards Service's, and the guidelines on how to conduct inspections and what to include in reports are not as extensive; arrangements are, on the whole, a good deal more ad hoc. On the other hand, headquarters people are in the field frequently, so that personal knowledge of conditions at the lowest administrative levels is continually refreshed.

Where the intensity of inspections is in the middle range, their

2. See Jerome T. Murphy, "Title I of ESEA: The Politics of Implementing Federal Education Reform," *Harvard Educational Review*, Vol. 41 (February 1971), pp. 35–63, especially pp. 39–43. See also Chap. 5, note 1, below.

value lies chiefly in verifying the products of the other modes of feedback and in protecting the integrity of the feedback system generally. In the stronger systems, inspections are also an important independent source of information and are employed as a device for training as well. Leaders of the agencies whose inspection practices are weak are reduced to faith in the accuracy of the other modes of feedback and in the desire and ability of subordinates to comply with what they think their superiors have directed.

Regardless of the state of their internal inspection systems, all of the agencies had in recent years been subject to inspections by *their* superiors that included visits to field stations at the lowest administrative levels. It is not often the case, however, that bureau headquarters learn from such inquiries much about their own lower ranks that they did not already know. On the contrary, a common objective of inspections by higher headquarters is to examine practices that bureau leaders may know perfectly well and would prefer not to have aired. Such inspections are more likely to embarrass the bureau leaders than to instruct them.

Still, there are occasions when such external inspections reveal important information to bureau officials. For example, the Bureau of Elementary and Secondary Education did not have a fully elaborated set of internal inspection practices, so an audit of state and local operations by examiners from the Audit Agency of the Department of Health, Education, and Welfare, which included studies in depth (and in the field) of many school districts, turned up evidence of noncompliance that would never have come up to the bureau leaders through the bureau feedback system then in effect.[3] Similarly, a General Accounting Office (GAO) review of uses to which Law Enforcement Assistance Administration funds were put by the beneficiaries disclosed a deviation the LEAA's own modest inspection capabilities at that time (1970–71) could not have revealed.[4] We saw no signs that these shortcomings had been

3. Murphy, "Title I of ESEA," pp. 44, 55.

4. Reported in *The Block Grant Programs of the Law Enforcement Assistance Administration*, Hearings before the Subcommittee on Legal and Monetary Affairs of the House Committee on Government Operations, 92 Cong. 1

known to the bureau's leaders, and we infer that their attention would not have been called to them when it was had there been no external inspections by higher authorities.

In all cases, furthermore, inspections from above—with their potential for embarrassing bureau leaders by exposing facts about their own agencies of which they themselves are ignorant—stimulate all bureaus to maintain their feedback systems in a state of good repair, and to improve them when possible. Thus, even when these inspections do not turn up anything the bureau leaders did not previously know, they influence internal feedback in the bureaus.

Since every bureau we looked at had been subjected to at least two such inspections in the last few years—some were inspected by the GAO, others by departmental examiners, still others by inspectors from levels between the bureaus and departments, and many by more than one of these—no bureaus are without this influence. They either get fresh feedback from the outside inspectors or are galvanized by the threat of external inspection (among other incentives) to assure themselves they are not ignorant of what goes on below.

The Web of Personal Contacts

Bureau leaders hear about their subordinates also from the network of personal communications found in every organization. It defies accurate and complete description. Moreover, since the information that passes through it is not recorded and subject to immediate review and verification or challenge, it is probably full of rumor, gossip, myth, fabrication, partial truth, error, and innuendo along with reliable data. We are therefore obliged to speak of the personal communications net in very general terms and with caution.

---

sess. (1971), Pt. 1, pp. 128–62. At the end of 1970, LEAA had a total of but 340 employees, only 60 of whom were not in Washington. As late as March 1971, very few audits of state programs had even begun. The capabilities of the Washington and regional offices have been steadily improved since then; by March 1972, total personnel had increased to 560, the audit staff had reached 40, and the auditing of the states was in a much higher gear.

There is evidence that this channel is impressively active, both downward and upward. In one bureau, for example, an official reported to us that he contrived a false memorandum describing some technical changes and "incidentally" announcing his own "transfer" to Alaska; by the end of the same day that he put it in his out-box, he began to get calls from friends in Albuquerque, a major field center of the organization. The news had traveled through the web of personal contacts faster than it could have moved through formal channels. Similarly, in another bureau, officials said that personnel decisions made in the central office commonly evoked reactions from the field before they were officially announced. The point is not that items were "leaked," but that knowledge of them spread via these informal pathways, and very swiftly.

Knowledge flows upward in corresponding fashion. In one agency Washington officers learned, even though it had not been officially reported to them, of a field agent's breach of a rule so basic that violation subjected the offender to formal charges and dismissal. Leaders of another agency established through informal means that some subordinates who certified they had complied with civil rights legislation were grossly exaggerating, to say the least. Civil servants enjoined by the regulations of still another bureau not to solicit endorsements of their work from their clienteles commonly ignored this rule, their superiors were informed by friends in the field. In another case, a field officer confessed to a Washington representative that official performance ratings of a colleague were made falsely favorable. In a regulatory bureau, everyone we talked to insisted it is known very quickly if an inspector "gets into bed with the operators" even though excessively sympathetic treatment or bending of the rules is not immediately apparent from the official records. That is not to say the bureaus are engaged in a continuous espionage effort; on the contrary, the information flows back without any systematic inquiry on the part of headquarters. The channels of personal communication leading in all directions function autonomously.

The channels consist of groups within the bureaus whose members maintain personal and usually trusting contact with one another even if they are geographically and organizationally dispersed. The groups do not seem to be very large, but there are many of them, and overlapping memberships link the pathways of communication in a web—or, more precisely, in several interconnected webs—reaching throughout the organizations.

The groups, like all groups, come together and stay together for a variety of reasons, and chance plays a large part in determining who is linked with whom. Two circumstances, however, appear particularly evident in the formation and continuation of such groups of personal friends and associates: shared experience and common strategic position.

People who enter an agency at the same time and go through their indoctrination and uneasy first days on the job together seem to form such ties. Those who serve together in the same office for a length of time also tend to sustain contacts as long as they remain in the same agency, no matter where. In fact, even those who go through short training courses together sometimes develop a kind of classmates' unity. When a man wants to find out something, apparently, he turns first to a friend he knows and trusts, or to a colleague who has reasons to hold the same views, or at least to someone who can be called by first name, and once the channels are opened they tend to encourage additional use that deepens and widens them. In all our bureaus, we found that people in headquarters could identify such contacts in many places in the organization.

We also found solidarity among occupational specialties and ideological allies. The oceanographers, photogrammetrists, and cartographers of the National Ocean Survey, for example, voice warm professional pride, and the sense of fraternity among their members (especially in competition with counterparts in other agencies, such as the Geological Survey) struck us as very strong; little goes on that affects their work or membership that is not known throughout their respective clans. Similarly, caseworkers who emphasize rehabilitation and guards who stress custody and discipline in prison management form separate social and professional groups, and personnel in headquarters coming out of either background find their friends in field stations helpful allies and sources of information. Ethnic identifications can have similar effects, so that Indians in the headquarters of the Bureau of Indian Affairs reach out to Indians in the field service—especially fellow tribesmen—in a very personal way; the "moccasin trail" (or the "moccasin telegraph") provides a swift channel.

Obviously, many of these contacts do not conform to organization charts; members of the groups reach out to each other across formally defined organizational levels and units. In that sense the web of personal contacts is to a large extent an informal communications network. But formal organizational practices and relationships also help to keep the contacts alive. For example, the Federal Telecommunications System, introduced in 1965, has so facilitated the flow of communications within and among administrative agencies—as indicated by Table 1—that it has richly nourished the opportunities for informal association. People can talk with each other personally very quickly and cheaply.

It is common practice in all our specimen bureaus for headquarters officers who have been to the field to brief their colleagues informally when they return, and field officers visiting headquarters invariably take pains to renew their personal associations with members of their groups as well as to perform their official duties. Rotation of personnel for training purposes and to prevent their capture by the local interests they serve or regulate helps establish and maintain such cohorts and to link them to headquarters when temporary duty in the central office is included in the program for executive development. Staff conferences between headquarters and field officials, facilitated by the general advancement of transportation and communications methods, are common; the administrator of the Federal Aviation Administration, for example, has a weekly conference telephone call with all his regional directors. The bureaus also encourage and even help professional staff to attend meetings of their relevant professional societies, thus bringing members of the various groups inside the organizations together with one another across lines of

TABLE 1

Intercity Telephone Calls on the Federal Telecommunications System
Compared with Federal Employment, 1965–72

Fiscal year	Calls per quarter (millions)[a]	Federal civilian employees (thousands)[b]
1965	9.0	2,539
1966	10.5	2,750
1967	11.6	2,956
1968	13.0	2,981
1969	15.7	3,006
1970	17.7	2,994
1971	20.5	2,852
1972	23.5	2,841

Sources: *Statistical Abstract of the United States*; and data supplied by the Statistical Control Branch, General Services Administration, and by the Civil Service Commission.

a. Figures for third quarter of 1965, first quarter of other years. Calls on separate military systems are excluded; the Department of Defense is a heavy user of the Federal Telecommunications System, however.

b. Average number per month, including intermittent employees but excluding Central Intelligence Agency and National Security Agency employees. For 1970, 1971, and 1972, figures represent the number in active-duty status as of March 31.

rank, administrative level, specialty, and level of government. The principal state-and-private forestry officer of the Forest Service even sits with the executive committee of the Association of American State Foresters, a means of maintaining relations highly useful for administrative feedback as well as for other purposes.

So the web of personal contacts is fashioned from both formal and informal elements. It therefore carries a great deal of traffic, including abundant cues and signals to bureau leaders about subordinate behavior.

Investigations

Far less frequently, feedback takes the form of an intensive investigation of an event that commands top-level attention in a

37

bureau or even higher. Whereas inspections are conducted routinely and are used for training as well as detection, investigations are triggered by specific events—disasters or scandals—and are usually characterized by efforts to assign responsibility. Investigations therefore occur much less frequently than inspections. In general, however, they make up in thoroughness what they lack in frequency.

No agency is immune to the kinds of events that provoke investigations. Four of our specimen bureaus are particularly vulnerable because disasters within their jurisdictions automatically attract attention from the mass media: a plane crash, a mine explosion, deaths from food poisoning, or a prison riot inevitably receive so much publicity that officials inside and outside the bureaus would be forced defensively to look into the causes even if they were not voluntarily inclined to; investigations in these cases are automatic. Marine and aeronautical accidents may also lead to examinations of the accuracy of navigational charts, and forest fires, even on state or private land, provoke questions of the Forest Service. But even the Bureau of Indian Affairs, the Bureau of Elementary and Secondary Education, and the Law Enforcement Assistance Administration, though not as susceptible to the shock of particular, isolated, dramatic events, work in areas where a concerned and committed constituency may at any time demand or conduct an intensive investigation. And any organization may find itself embroiled in scandal if it is not constantly careful.

A vivid illustration of the relevance of investigations for administrative feedback, provided during the course of our study, was the congressional investigation of an explosion in a Kentucky coal mine that killed thirty-eight miners.[5] The subcommittee

5. *Investigation of the Hyden, Kentucky, Coal Mine Disaster of December 30, 1970*, Report of the General Subcommittee on Labor of the House Committee on Education and Labor, 92 Cong. 1 sess. (1971). Also see James Westfield, *Official Report of Major Mine Explosion Disaster, Nos. 15 and 16 Mines, Finley Coal Company, Hyden, Leslie County, Kentucky*, U.S. Bureau of Mines (1971); Ward Sinclair, "Inspectors Missed Blast-Ripped Mine," *Washington Post*, Jan. 1, 1971, and "Mine Blast Fallout: Misery Mounts for Inspector Who Checked Disaster Site," *Louisville Courier-Journal*, March

report, critical of the Bureau of Mines (and sharply challenged in a minority report by seven of the subcommittee's sixteen members), addressed itself in great detail to the behavior of the bureau's safety inspectors. The inspectors' activities day by day were reviewed in the testimony and in the report. The quality of their inspections was evaluated. The relationships between one of the inspectors and the mine owner were examined minutely. In the end, no evidence of impropriety was unearthed. But a spotlight had been turned on the work of subordinate personnel that lifted it from obscurity and subjected it to the most searching inquiry.

Did this investigation alert the central office of the bureau to behavior of which it would otherwise not have been aware? That is not certain. The bureau conducted its own investigation, as any agency does when something drastically out of the ordinary takes place; moreover, both the administrative and the congressional investigations depended heavily on official records routinely filed by subordinates. It is unlikely, therefore, that the legislative inquiry disclosed anything the bureau had not already found out for itself, particularly since legislative review could be anticipated. But the difference in the perspectives and interests of the congressmen clearly led to questions and interpretations not identical with those generated within the bureau. To this extent, fresh viewpoints on subordinate performance were fed back, though they did not in this instance oblige headquarters to revise its picture of field behavior.

This episode is not the sort of thing that happens every day. But it illustrates how crises can precipitate investigations in which subordinate behavior becomes the focus of attention and the subject of intensive administrative feedback.

Centralized Services

Still another way headquarters learn of subordinate behavior is by taking over activities that would otherwise have to be per-

---

12, 1971; George Velsey, "Mine Inspector Queried on Blast" and "Mine Owner on Stand as Inquiry Ends," *New York Times*, March 10 and 14, 1971.

formed in the field. The Forest Service, for example, by compiling and analyzing the reports on assistance to private woodland owners and wood processors, is more quickly and better apprised of patterns in the field than are many of the state officials and field operators. Similarly, in the National Ocean Survey, data collected by teams on ships are stored on magnetic tapes and brought to regional headquarters, where computers plot the soundings on charts. In the Federal Aviation Administration the Office of General Counsel takes charge of all dockets established when agency officers, such as the field personnel of the Flight Standards Service, take action against a client (a pilot, say, or an airline, or a repair service) that might require legal action in the administrative or judicial arenas. In the Bureau of Mines, penalties for violations of safety laws and regulations may be assessed only by the Office of Assessment and Compliance Assistance in Washington, a practice that obliges some of the headquarters staff to examine what goes on in the field. The Bureau of Foods, the Bureau of Prisons, and the Bureau of Mines were, at the time of our study, in the process of adding computer services to their central statistical services.

There is no question that the services are real and relieve field staffs of some chores they would otherwise have to perform themselves. Still, the practice means that subordinates feed to higher levels detailed information that would otherwise be summarized, conveying only selected data. When subordinates provide the facts on which a penalty for a safety violation will be based, or a formal adjudicatory docket will be built, or a calculation of agency output will be made, they inevitably tell their central offices a great deal about themselves.

To be sure, there are also tendencies toward decentralization. In the Flight Standards Service, for example, new safety-enforcement procedures were adopted to free field personnel from the time-consuming record-keeping required to build a formal docket, and to release legal counsel from routine processing of dockets; field officers were granted some discretion in handling prohibited practices, without always preparing to punish them formally. But centralized services, particularly since the advent of the computer, are still very much in evidence and constitute a substantial component of administrative feedback wherever they appear.

Even though the network of personal communications turned out to occupy a more important position than we anticipated in the array of methods by which leaders get intelligence about the activities of their subordinates, the general feedback pattern did not really surprise us. The principal modes of administrative feedback coincide roughly with prevailing management doctrine.

We were surprised, however, by the comparative inactivity of three sources we had expected would play much larger parts in systems of administrative feedback than they actually do. We surmised the bureaus' clienteles, their employees, and the communications media would provide much more information about subordinates than is the case. They do perform this service, to be sure, but at a much lower level of intensity than we reasoned they would.

Clients

Take the clienteles of the bureaus, for example. At the start of the study it seemed reasonable to suppose that their objections to decisions adverse to their wishes and interests would furnish a steady stream of clues to how subordinates were acting. Even if the charges were unfounded, they would still be useful because accusations shown to be false would assure leaders that their subordinates were adhering to policy.

Headquarters do hear from clients. Most people do not write the bureaus directly. Far more frequently they address themselves to their congressmen. They also write the President or cabinet officers or other high administrators. The staffs of these officials forward the missives to the appropriate agencies. Eventually, therefore, most of them come down to the bureaus.

The volume of such communications depends on many factors, including the size of the clienteles, the impact of agency decisions

41

on the lives of the clients, the attention given the agencies in public statements of visible public figures and in the mass media, and the comprehensibility of the agencies' work. So in any given year the Food and Drug Administration is likely to get several thousand communications, the Bureau of Elementary and Secondary Education something on the same order, the Bureau of Indian Affairs somewhat less, but still a large number. At the other end of the scale, excepting requests for publications, the National Ocean Survey measures its clientele communications in hundreds rather than thousands, and still fewer communications affecting the Forest Service bear directly on the activities of the state and private forestry program. But all receive some communications from the public.

Nevertheless, what impressed us was that the overwhelming bulk of the communications were first-instance requests or inquiries that should have been addressed directly to field offices rather than to higher headquarters or political intermediaries, or were commentaries on general policies rather than information about subordinates. The Bureau of Mines, in an effort to encourage the flow of real information from clients, installed a "hot line" permitting informants to make toll free (and, if they wish, anonymous) calls to the bureau's Washington office to report safety violations (thus exposing laxity or oversights on the part of mine inspectors). After a few calls, the system fell into disuse. It was reactivated at the insistence of a U.S. senator, but bureau officials claimed it had been uninformative.[6] Whatever the reasons, the fact is that clients expose surprisingly little in the agencies we studied.

Even though we found no specific illustrations, it seems probable that citizen reports on violations of the law by other *citizens* will occasionally reveal something headquarters thinks a regular employee *should* have prevented or corrected or at least detected. And we have evidence that reports by clients alert leaders to devia-

6. But one reporter located a miner who said his valid complaint through the hot line had been ignored. Ward Sinclair, "Report on Mine Hot-Line Failure Disputed," *Louisville Courier-Journal*, Feb. 5, 1972.

tions from intended policies by *subordinates*, as in the case of complaints from parents and private-school administrators in some areas that private schools were not receiving fair shares of Title I funds, which led to corrective instructions being issued to the responsible officers in the field. Moreover, the Bureau of Prisons keeps a Prisoners' Mail Box in each of its facilities, and prisoners are advised they may write to public officials in all three branches of government in the states and in Washington (whose names and addresses are posted) with assurance that their letters will be mailed unopened. (Eventually, though, letters to the director of the bureau, or to other officials who send them to the director with requests for explanation or remedial action, are placed in the inmates' files.) When we say that client communications are more rarely a source of information about the administrative behavior of subordinates than we expected, we do not mean to imply they are invariably absent or totally ineffective. But as a channel of administrative feedback they are of minor significance.

We also thought bureau headquarters would learn a great deal about subordinate behavior from formal proceedings instituted by clients seeking to overturn lower-level decisions running against them. We did not expect such proceedings by individual citizens against the *intergovernmental* agencies because the normal line of action in such cases would run to the state and local agencies receiving federal moneys, and in fact this turned out to be the case. But we thought the story would be different in the directly administered programs. Indians have many grievances and a long history of court suits. The powers of regulatory bureaus have likewise generated numerous legal actions. (The Food and Drug Administration actually has few powers over food processors, having either to go to court to compel action or to rely on warning letters. But the Bureau of Mines can close mines and assess penalties, and the Federal Aviation Administration can revoke and suspend licenses and impose fines.) The inmates of prisons have recently been resorting with increasing frequency to formal adjudicatory actions. And even the National Ocean Survey has been the target of court suits by users of their maps who once in a while claim damages because of alleged errors in the Survey's charts (claims never yet found to have merit). We therefore anticipated that appeals and suits would constantly call to the attention of the agency leaders how subordinates were doing their jobs.

It turns out, however, that while the threat of formal proceedings against bureaus restrains administrative tendencies toward arbitrary action, the proceedings themselves seldom inform leaders in the bureaus about occurrences at lower levels that they do not know long before the formal stage is reached. For one thing, small bureaus do not have elaborate internal appeals procedures; formal administrative appeals lie to administrative officers or special external panels above the bureaus, who are treated as the decision-making authority. Thus, when appealable actions are taken, staff at headquarters are automatically involved in the process before the actions take effect. The Office of the General Counsel of the Federal Aviation Administration and the Office of Assessment and Compliance Assistance in the Bureau of Mines are examples. And when an agency must go to *court* for compulsory process, as the Food and Drug Administration must to enforce its orders to food processors, its leaders must be prepared to defend its requests for court support, so they are drawn immediately into such decisions.

Second, the mere possibility that certain kinds of decisions of the bureaus may have to be defended in external arenas leads to special care in establishing records and submitting reports to headquarters. Consequently, especially in the regulatory agencies, the Washington offices almost always have ongoing reports of such developments. To be sure, hardly any individual case gets extensive attention until it does begin to ripen into a formal proceeding. But the formal proceeding is not what first brings the information to headquarters; it merely alerts people at the center to focus on the available data. The process of appeal usually tells leaders about the state of mind of the appellant rather than revealing new information about behavior of subordinates.

Third, such a minute number of decisions ordinarily reach the stage of formal proceedings that they do not really constitute a significant sample of the total range of subordinate actions. The Bureau of Mines was an exception at the time we studied it because mine operators routinely appealed from the majority of fines imposed by the bureau when they discovered the appeals machinery was backlogged and they could delay indefinitely the actual collection of the money. But only in Mines was this the case, and even there the appeals lay from the decisions of the headquarters Office of Assessment and Compliance Assistance (in the name of the bureau) to an interdepartmental Appeals Panel, so the appeals did not add any information to the leaders' existing knowledge about subordinates. In none of our specimens are appeals an important mode of administrative feedback.

That is not to say appeals are unimportant in all respects. On the contrary, it is clear that the leaders and members of the bureaus tend to use their powers with restraint and caution when there is a chance they will have to defend their actions before external tribunals. But requirements and procedures can have profound impact on what administrators do without adding significantly to administrative feedback about subordinates. That is the case with respect to formal appeals proceedings.

We were also surprised by how seldom groups purporting to represent clients raise questions about subordinate behavior. We anticipated that these groups would call attention to subordinates they considered excessively zealous or lax, or too high-handed, or too accommodating to special interests (other than their own). And, indeed, "case work" for members is one of the chores they perform. Nevertheless, their principal concern turns out to be policy, not the behavior of individual subordinates. They are much more interested in the *provisions* of directives than in the actions of subordinates who do not comply with them. The net result is that bureau leaders hear much more from these groups about legislation and general regulations than about the activities of personnel at lower levels. These "intercessor groups" seem hardly ever to provide much administrative feedback.

All the same, we did discover two instances in which they did—both of them in bureaus that function intergovernmentally and that did not at that time have well-developed feedback about the uses made by recipients of the funds they distributed. Studies published by a number of groups disclosed applications of Title I money by local school authorities that allegedly violated the terms under which funds were granted.[7] The Urban Coalition similarly challenged some of the expenditures of state and local law enforcement officers made possible by grants from the Law Enforcement Assistance Administration.[8] In both instances, the complainants conducted their own original field inquiries.

But we did not come across comparable cases in the other seven agencies. Feedback about subordinate behavior is not one of the contributions to administration for which their clientele associations are likely to stand out.

The Communications Media

Neither will the communications media stand out in this respect. Given the specialized jurisdiction of the bureaus, it is not surprising that the mass media do not give space to the behavior of lower level personnel. It seemed plausible, however, that trade journals, or union organs, or the specialized press, or technical periodicals, or the applicable professional journals would turn their spotlights on the lower levels.[9] But they did not while we were conducting our study.

7. Washington Research Project and NAACP Legal Defense and Educational Fund, Inc., *Title I of ESEA: Is It Helping Poor Children?* (2d ed.; Washington: Washington Research Project and NAACP Legal Defense and Educational Fund, 1969); NAACP Legal Defense and Educational Fund, Inc., *An Even Chance: A Report on Federal Funds for Indian Children in Public School Districts* (New York: NAACP Legal Defense and Educational Fund, 1971); National Committee on the Education of Migrant Children, *Wednesday's Children: A Report on Programs Funded Under the Migrant Amendment to Title I of the Elementary and Secondary Education Act* (New York: National Committee on the Education of Migrant Children, 1971).

8. National Urban Coalition, "Law and Disorder I" (Washington, 1970; processed).

9. Publications of this type, which presuppose special knowledge on the part of readers, are able to discuss details of law, administration, and relevant advocacy. In many cases they act or aspire to act as spokesmen for group interests, and they emphasize vigilance over all developments that

It is not that the bureaus do not receive attention; all have been the subjects of news stories or features in one place or another. But the journalists focus on their programs, or the high politics forming their policies, or the sparring and footwork of political maneuvering. There is hardly ever an examination of subordinate behavior that would instruct leaders.

It happens now and then, of course. For example, the *Louisville Courier-Journal*, which takes special pains to cover the coal mining industry, revealed that a former foreman in a mine that blew up as a result of using prohibited forms of explosive had been hired by a district office of the Bureau of Mines as an inspector.[10] Astonished headquarters officials quickly reversed the local action. And one of the articles treating questionable applications of Title I funds appeared in the *Harvard Educational Review*.[11] *Life* magazine ran a long story on staff handling of an inmate in one of the institutions of the Bureau of Prisons[12] (done, however, with the knowledge

---

affect their clienteles. Particularly in the regulatory areas, federal agency activities initiate a very large share of the "news." A few of the specialized journals pertinent to the agencies in our sample are: *Food Plant Ideas* (issued bimonthly at Minneapolis); *Food Engineering* (monthly, Philadelphia); *Aerospace Maintenance* (monthly, San Bernardino, Calif.); *Aviation Week and Space Technology* (weekly, New York); *NEA Journal* (monthly, Washington: National Education Association); *Sierra Club Bulletin* (monthly, San Francisco); *Virginia Forests* (quarterly, Richmond); *American Journal of Correction* (bimonthly, St. Paul); *Police Chief* (monthly, Gaithersburg, Md.); *Navaho Times* (weekly, Window Rock, Ariz.); *United Mine Workers Journal* (semimonthly, Washington); *Independent Coal Operator* (monthly, Middlesboro, Ky.); *Geo-Marine Technology* (monthly, Washington); *Navigation* (quarterly, Morristown, N.J.).

10. Ward Sinclair, "Mine Bureau Official Upset by Hiring of Hyden Inspector," *Louisville Courier-Journal*, June 26, 1971. The paper quoted a high official in the Bureau of Mines: "I damn near fell out of my chair. . . . It's the most incredible thing I've ever heard of—and I've heard a lot of incredible things the last two years."

11. Murphy, "Title I of ESEA."

12. Denny Walsh, "The Gorilla Cowed His Keepers," *Life*, June 25, 1971. See also letter from Norman A. Carlson, director of the Bureau of Prisons, and reply by Walsh, *Life*, Aug. 20, 1971; and interview with P. J. Ciccone, director of the institution in question, "Konigsberg Very Difficult, Treated Him Humanely . . ." *Springfield* (Mo.) *Leader and Press*, June 21, 1971.

and cooperation of bureau headquarters, which had voluminous records on the handling of this prisoner long before the reporter began his research). The *Washington Post* printed numerous stories about prison practices based on interviews with the inmates.[13] So it is not unknown for the communications media to pick up something illuminating the activities of subordinates. But not more than once in a great while.

Moreover, the occasional stories about administrative practice at the lowest organizational levels seldom deal with this subject in a way that will enlighten experienced and knowledgeable agency leaders. Usually, they are aimed at outsiders—perhaps to stir them to action, perhaps to entertain them, perhaps merely as filler on a dull day, perhaps for other purposes. Indeed, factions within bureaucracies commonly are the sources of stories about agencies; the "exposé" is frequently a strategic airing of facts well known within the bureaus.[14] So even when the communications media focus on the administrative behavior of subordinates, they seldom tell leaders much they had not already learned through internal channels.

Zealous or Disaffected Employees

We had also expected—and, indeed, were often told—that subordinate employees themselves would let headquarters know when their fellows had stepped out of line and all local efforts to control them had failed. Through the medium of the suggestion box, perhaps, or confidential complaints, or even through open denunciation, presumably violators of the rules would be revealed to leaders. The motivations for tattling, obviously, are not necessarily—or even usually—lofty, but it is true that dedication to program or principle will often inspire such a move, even if risk to the informer is a consequence. At any rate, the very diversity of

13. See Ben H. Bagdikian, *The Shame of the Prisons* (Simon and Schuster, 1972); the series first appeared in the *Washington Post*, Jan. 30–Feb. 6, 1972.
14. Leon V. Sigal, "Bureaucratic Objectives and Tactical Use of the Press: Why Bureaucrats Leak" (paper presented at 1971 meeting of the American Political Science Association; processed).

motives that could lead to exposure increases expectations such action will occur frequently.

In the nine bureaus we studied, it occurs very rarely. In only one case we know of did headquarters learn of subordinate departures from policy through the complaints of a subordinate's fellow employees (other than inspectors); a prison guard who maltreated some prisoners was reported by a colleague. He did so, however, only after an investigation, undertaken as a result of suspicions aroused by other feedback, had gone on for some time, and when he was under intense questioning by a member of the bureau's legal staff. What is more, he burst into tears when he informed. Employees may have all kinds of ways of preventing proscribed action and compelling required action on the part of their co-workers, but informing to higher headquarters is apparently not ordinarily one of them. They do not tell on one another. This theoretical pipeline runs dry in actuality.

THE CHARACTER OF FEEDBACK ABOUT COMPLIANCE

Despite the silence of many of the theoretical modes of feedback, a plenitude of data about subordinate behavior does indeed reach headquarters in most cases. Seven of the nine bureau offices in Washington clearly receive a great deal of information from which it is possible to detect patterns of noncompliance among their subordinates.

That is not to say the information thrusts itself on their consciousness; on the contrary, detection usually requires deliberate, intensive search and analysis by those in the top ranks. Nor is the evidence the kind that would stand up in court as decisive; most of it is circumstantial, and what it establishes is inferred rather than directly demonstrated. Further, not all the data point in the same direction; often, conflicts and ambiguities render the meaning hard to discern. Finally, not all the signals and messages that reach the top levels are accurate and reliable; the quality is uneven.

But information is at hand, and in ample quantity. A headquarters staff so inclined can, in our judgment, sift it for guidance

about the degree of compliance with policy on the part of subordinates in seven of the nine bureaus we studied. There will be
lacunae in their information. There will be uncertainty about
whether compliance leads to achievement of goals. In broad terms,
however, the feedback system furnishes an adequate basis for
leadership groups to determine whether their subordinates are
within acceptable limits in their official actions.

The two exceptions are the Law Enforcement Assistance Administration and the Bureau of Elementary and Secondary Education (BESE). To say this is not to call them delinquent. As
distributors of funds to agencies and subdivisions of sovereign
governments, they do not regard as subordinates the recipients of
grants prescribed by statute. BESE explicitly eschewed a role as
monitor and relied almost exclusively on the plans of applicants,
submitted with their applications, to judge whether field behavior
conformed to requirements. LEAA similarly depended heavily on
state officials to monitor lower levels, with very little direct verification of what was happening on the ground. The way in which
these bureaus interpreted their responsibilities may be challenged,
but the interpretations certainly can be, and are, defended. At any
rate, as a result of these views, these bureaus did not develop the
kind of feedback about field behavior that the others in our sample
did, and they therefore did not have at their disposal in their
headquarters at the time of our study the kind of information
about compliance that the others had.

To call them exceptions, of course, is to imply a norm they fall
outside of. In this sense, they are exceptions that test a rule, but in
our view they do not overturn it, because most of the agencies we
studied had enough feedback to permit detection of the general
outlines of noncompliance at even the lowest levels.

The stream of feedback clearly does not flow like the beam of a
television tube, projecting an easily discernible image that anyone
sitting before the screen can comprehend at once. It consists of
many disparate bits demanded by many different people for many
unrelated uses, not to mention purely fortuitous data. There is no
integrated pattern in their timing or content or form. They are not

all directed to the same place in headquarters, nor are they systematically displayed on a single board that relates them logically to one another. And even if they were put together they would not compose a coherent picture; they would constitute a collection of fragments from which the patterns would have to be inferred. To an even greater extent than most perceptions of shape and meaning, interpretations of the messages fed back to headquarters about the day-by-day behavior of subordinates depend on the sensitivity of the interpreters to configurations (or gestalts) suggested by the fragments.

To have served in the lowest administrative echelons is a great advantage in understanding the symbols; the experience permits the remote administrator immediately to visualize the situation below. Gestalts of this kind are learned patterns, and a glimpse of a fraction is often sufficient to summon up the entire pattern. This is one advantage of serving in the field before going to headquarters.

Experience in the bureaus helps top-level staff in another way: it enables them to evaluate the sources of much of the data received, to appreciate the motivations and objectives of subordinates who originate and transmit the data. Knowing who tends to exaggerate and who to understate the problems, who panics easily and who is too complacent, equips leaders to discount some signals and investigate others, to read more intelligently the heterogenous indicators of what their subordinates are doing. Old hands are educated to the styles and the strengths and the foibles of many of their colleagues, and this background hones their perceptiveness in using administrative feedback.

In over half the bureaus and programs studied, even the heads of the agencies or programs and their lieutenants were seasoned in this way. The Bureau of Indian Affairs brought in outsiders at the top; the Law Enforcement Assistance Administration was a quite new agency; the Bureau of Mines and the Bureau of Foods reached out for new blood. Regardless of the composition of the very top layer, however, the central offices of every bureau comprise many old hands who worked their way up from lower levels over the years (and, in some of the intergovernmental agencies, who had

had state or local experience). While none was staffed this way *exclusively*, all had a substantial leavening of such veterans in the Washington office—and, in our judgment, relied heavily on them, though sometimes reluctantly.

This means every bureau has, at least theoretically, a capacity to piece together a fairly complete picture of what goes on below even when the feedback is far from comprehensive and authenticated. In every case there are people who are able to perceive a great deal of subordinate behavior from incomplete, piecemeal, scattered bits of information.

Thus we may say that the combined effect of the various modes of feedback is synergistic—the whole is greater than the sum of the individual effects of each. The concatenation of sources is such that each illuminates and amplifies the others, exposing actions that might otherwise escape notice and calling attention to patterns that might otherwise remain obscure. The fact that some channels are very seldom used does not mean they are useless; their existence adds to the impact of the more commonly employed ones. If we assume the total likelihood and extent of noncompliance are curbed by the probability of detection, then the multiplicity of feedback mechanisms contributes more than negligibly to restraining noncompliance by raising that probability. Looking at each mode and channel of feedback separately may therefore give a wrong impression of the general result; the whole fabric of the system must be considered as an entity. That is why executives are not inclined to worry about the tendencies toward noncompliance in spite of the havoc they could cause.

But their confidence, in turn, sometimes leads to astonishment and disappointment when the feedback process seems to fail them and things do not work out as they expected. Despite the undeniable power of administrative feedback, the process has built into it distinct limits that circumscribe its success.

IV

The Limits of Feedback

DESPITE the abundance of feedback detail, the synergistic effects of the several modes of feedback, and collective experience of headquarters staffs in interpreting data, there is reason to believe a great deal goes on at lower levels that the leaders do not find out about. No feedback system picks up everything. Chances are, given the limits of feedback, no system ever will—or can.

LEADERS SHUN DETAILS

One reason is so obvious and familiar as to need no elaboration: the cost of collecting and digesting information. When the benefits from acquiring an additional increment of feedback are exceeded by the cost, going after that increment makes little sense. Hence, holding down costs is always a factor in designing feedback systems. Perhaps that is why all the systems have at least one feature in common: they are essentially a complex of alarms designed to sound when samples of certain selected aspects of subordinate behavior exceed established limits. They are quality-control arrangements aimed at the quality of subordinate behavior.

Quality control, especially of this kind, is an ordering of triggers, tolerances, and trust. The more trust the designers of a feedback complex have in the subordinates to be monitored, the broader the tolerances within which the subordinates are permitted to function without surveillance; they are subject to fewer specifications, fewer constraints. Broader tolerances, in turn, mean "wider spacing" of the triggers—that is, accommodation of greater variation in behavior before a trigger is tripped and an alarm set off.

The narrower the tolerances and the more sensitive the triggers, the more costly a complex of alarms is likely to be. It generates more data to sift through than does a less stringent system. It goes off more often, requiring more investigations and inquiries. It results in slower, more cautious work by subordinates, and more frequent checks with their superiors. It obliges executives to divert their attention and energies from strategic problems of policy and of external relations to details of internal operations. In short, it absorbs a higher proportion of organizational resources than do less demanding alarm systems, thereby raising costs.

We would therefore expect leaders to set the tolerances as broad as they dare and as the law permits. In practice, they commonly divide responsibility, creating units with crosscutting jurisdictions that must come to terms with one another in order to complete their work, thus introducing an element of automatic mutual restraint into their organizations. But restraints slow down production and increase costs even when they are automatic. The desire to know what is happening below, and to control and restrain thus wars in each executive with his desire to keep his own time free for policy matters, with his wish not to be submerged in administrative detail, and with his preference for high output and low cost. The optimal strategy for the average executive would therefore be to loosen tolerance to the point where he is alerted only to serious threats to organizational survival and his own position.

As indicated by the volume of reports each bureau requires, this optimum is not achieved in all agencies in all respects.[1] Nevertheless, many triggers in feedback systems do seem to be set further apart than they could be, allowing many organization leaders to ignore what goes on below until it develops possibilities of disastrous consequences. If the organization proceeds on its present course without much controversy or danger, leaders are not apt to probe its inner workings at lowest levels; they seldom seek out this kind of trouble. They are more inclined to focus on what they regard as larger matters.

1. See pp. 25ff., above.

To be sure, in excluding data, leaders often make what they themselves would admit are mistakes. They sometimes misgauge the way their subordinates will employ discretion. They forget that tolerances suited to one set of conditions may be inapplicable to another; if the clientele of an agency changes, for example, or if the clients discover loopholes in the laws and regulations, or if a technology is modified, subordinates might adapt in ways never anticipated when broad areas were left to their personal judgment. (To illustrate, when the racial composition of a clientele shifts, or when a previously docile clientele grows aggressive in the pursuit of its interests, old assumptions about the conduct of subordinates and the latitude appropriately granted them may be totally invalidated.)

Nevertheless, even though organizations may make bad choices or may allow sound choices to become obsolete, it is still true that conscious intent is one of the reasons feedback systems exclude certain kinds of information. They *deliberately* incorporate some gaps of information that is regarded as unnecessary for the proper discharge of managerial responsibility. It is partly a matter of design.

THE BOUNDS OF RECEPTIVITY

Quite apart from deliberate avoidance of excessive sounding of the alarms about subordinate behavior, some factors circumscribe leadership receptivity to such signals when they do sound. Alarm signals may be screened out because they sound constantly, or they may be drowned out by competing signals, or they may be discredited. Consequently, though they may clang insistently, they may attract no attention from leaders.

Screened-out Signals

Sheer repetition can reduce the effectiveness of alarms; any repeated stimulus, we know, gradually loses its force. Because there are so many channels and modes of feedback, even though most of them are seldom active and the major ones themselves are intermittent, and even though a good deal of variation is tolerated at lower levels, it must seem to each headquarters as though a message about subordinates is being received somewhere in the Washington office all the time. In a way, the continuing crackling is like the dial tone in a telephone—an indication that the system is in a state of readiness. Yet it would be surprising if hearing it so unendingly did not dull the receptivity of the listeners.

Another reason leaders seem often to filter out signals is that they neither requested nor want some of the data flowing back to headquarters. Figures on the distribution of services by congressional districts, or of agency personnel by grades, or other information designed to serve congressional purposes may not coincide with agency management goals. Some reports originate to satisfy requirements of governmentwide overhead agencies (the Office of Management and Budget, for instance, or the Civil Service Commission), of departmental control offices, or occasionally even the White House. A few get started under one set of bureau leaders and continue because nobody takes the trouble to review them and terminate the ones that have outlived their usefulness. Collectively, such data contribute to a communications overload for executives, who must decide which inputs to consider and which to ignore. Naturally, they tend to screen out materials thrust on them by others. In so doing they may cast out wheat as well as chaff, but unless they limit their receptivity they may be overwhelmed.[2] The alternatives leave them little real choice.

We could not confirm empirically that such a diminution of receptivity does occur. We have little doubt, however, that the repetition and the overload often associated with such a diminution

2. See the testimony of James R. Schlesinger in *Planning, Programming, Budgeting,* Inquiry of the Subcommittee on National Security and International Operations for the Senate Committee on Government Operations, 91 Cong. 1 sess. (1970), p. 482: "What happened in Vietnam is that we were simply drowned in statistics; we were drowned in information. A very small proportion of this information was adequately analyzed. We would have been much better off to have a much smaller take of information and to have done a better job of interpreting what that information meant."

do occur in the bureau headquarters we looked at, especially those with steadily and steeply rising work loads. It is therefore plausible that some signals of noncompliance by subordinates are over-looked for these reasons, and, indeed, that there is a rising threshold of filtration of such warning signals over time. This means the degree of deviation from the intent of the leaders, the extent of danger to the organization, and the strength of the signals will all have to increase constantly and substantially to be noticed—that is, the tolerances of deviation are steadily broadening. Thus, tol-erances of deviation may expand without anyone consciously will-ing the expansion.

Drowned-out Signals

Signals about subordinate behavior are only one kind of intelli-gence about the performance and condition of a bureau that reaches its leadership group. Some of the others enjoy, and perhaps de-mand, higher priority. For instance, all our agencies find them-selves under pressure from one external group or another to alter their announced policies; that is almost universal. Most are under budgetary pressure as well. Some have to defend their jurisdic-tional boundaries; the Bureau of Indian Affairs, for example, has occasionally been beset by bureaucratic rivals who would parcel out its programs among themselves. Congressional, White House, and secretarial displeasure are hazards bureau leaders worry about and try to prevent. Admittedly, exposure of noncompliant be-havior of subordinates would handicap any bureau in any or all of these relationships, so the incentives for bureaus to guard against it are strong. As long as the feedback system suggests subordinate actions are within tolerable boundaries, however, bureau leaders apply themselves almost exclusively to the other problems. Feed-back about subordinates gets short shrift in inner circles when it competes with those matters. It is generally among the less urgent of the leaders' worries, which sets a limit on their receptivity to it.

Discredited Signals

Anyone outside an organization charging that subordinate

personnel are not complying with the directives of the leaders presumably knows the content, the purpose, and thrust of the directives. As we have seen, such charges from outside a bureau are far from common. When they *are* made, however, they are often based on interpretations favoring the complainant's special interests. Sometimes they spring from faulty information about what the directives provide and are intended to accomplish. So, unless the source's competence is recognized promptly, the first response to such an accusation is to pass it along to lower levels where a routine explanation of the action is drafted. Even accusations transmitted by congressmen are handled this way.

This practice quiets most complainants (whether or not it satisfies them), which reinforces the practice. After all, if routine explanations are enough to take care of most such complaints, charges of noncompliance having *real* merit (or *strong* motivations behind them) would seem extraordinarily rare. So a kind of taint of invalidity or frivolousness attaches presumptively to all such complaints, and not many are likely to overcome this handicap sufficiently to attract serious high-level consideration. The negative presumption muffles the signals.

Another reason complaints of this nature are frequently rejected as prima facie evidence of a pattern of subordinate noncompliance is the presumption that only the disgruntled are ordinarily motivated to take the trouble to communicate. Since the number of communiqués related to subordinate behavior is small relative to the total number of transactions between organizations and the people they deal with, leaders who subscribe to the belief that they hear only the squeaking wheels give only passing notice to what is construed as a severely biased sample. To be sure, an extraordinary surge of denunciation might provoke high-level concern and an organizational response, but bureau headquarters, like congressional offices, try to discriminate between widespread spontaneous outcries and mobilized campaigns, and between well-grounded complaints and spurious ones (such as the stream of letters that poured into the Food and Drug Administration after reports of mercury contamination of tuna, in some of which people alleged they opened cans of tuna and found them loaded with mercury). Thus, even a burst of signals may be discredited.

We do not suggest bureau headquarters are uniformly deaf to evidence of subordinates' misbehavior. What we are saying is that in spite of all that feedback has going for it, it is limited in its success because leadership receptivity is far from total.

FRAGMENTATION OF HEADQUARTERS

Let headquarters be as receptive as possible and as attentive to detail as they can, and all our bureaus will *still* experience limitations in their feedback systems because each Washington office is a collection of specialists who focus on their own areas of expertise rather than a homogenous body in which all incoming intelligence diffuses uniformly. Bits of information that would promptly alert leaders to problems of noncompliance if they were placed side by side feed into different components of the central offices, each of which concentrates on one part of the total operation and ignores others except as the work of the others impinges directly on its own. So the data in many cases are not juxtaposed. Headquarters fragmentation thus offsets in part the ability of high officials to perceive large patterns from small clues. More information is available in headquarters than is efficiently collated and analyzed.

Thus, for example, a member of the Food and Drug Administration's Office of Compliance declared that he sent the commissioner and associate commissioner full information about an investigation of a possibly contaminated medical product; but when a journalist reported they denied knowing about it, he replied, "I report things and I write memos. But someone above me makes the decisions about who sees them."[3] In like fashion, a reporter for the *Wall Street Journal* confronted the director of the Bureau of Mines, who had taken the position only nine months earlier, with evidence that his Office of Assessment and Compliance Assistance was assessing fines for coal mine safety violations

3. Robert J. Bazell, "Food and Drug Administration: Is Protecting Lives a Priority?" *Science*, Vol. 172 (April 2, 1971), p. 42.

that were far below the published schedule of penalties for such offenses (the office is part of the headquarters structure). The director, according to the reporter, "seems uncertain about the details of his bureau's assessment program" and "professes ignorance" of the low fines. " 'I'll look into it,' he promises. 'Maybe that's something we shouldn't be doing.' "[4] Having data in headquarters, clearly, is not the same as having knowledge of the data, thanks partly to the fragmentation of staff.

GROUP SOLIDARITY

Another limit on feedback is the identification of organization members with each other. Identification of this kind is a complex psychological phenomenon, including elements of individual self-interest ("If I don't expose them when I see them getting out of line, they won't expose me in similar situations") and collective defensiveness (disclosing noncompliance by colleagues may provide materials for an organization's critics and foes even though the disclosure is meant only for internal use). But it is also compounded of honor, loyalty, commitment to program, compassion, and similar altruistic motives. At any rate, whatever their motivations, the members of groups often do tend to support and protect one another rather than to inform on each other.[5]

This being the case, bureau members might well yield to temptations not to tell higher levels about observed noncompliance at their own levels; in one bureau such a case of suppressed noncompliance did surface. To be sure, suppression is not always

4. Burt Schorr, *Wall Street Journal*, July 28, 1971.
5. Thus, when the police commissioner of New York City urged policemen to report instances of corruption in the department directly to him, to district attorneys, or to the Department of Investigation, a survey of members of the force disclosed most of them would report only to their precinct commanders. "The man who's important to us," said one patrolman, "is the commander. . . . He's the man we know. He's the man we trust." Another declared, "It'd be like ratting on your buddies. Look, your commanding officer is a guy you can explain things to, really talk to." Robert D. McFadden, *New York Times*, May 18, 1970.

the same as ignoring or approving such behavior. On the contrary, corporate or professional pride engenders all sorts of informal techniques of social control intended to prevent or correct it; after all, persistent noncompliance can be as harmful to a group as disclosures made for the purpose of terminating such behavior. But while members keep each other in line, and the deterrent effect of such informal, mutual restraint at lower levels may be even greater than more complete feedback to higher headquarters would be, the higher levels can never be sure they are getting the full story about what goes on day by day in the lower reaches of their organizations. It is in this sense that group solidarity may limit feedback.

If informal, mutual control can be as successful in discouraging subordinate noncompliance with headquarters directives as is headquarters policing, leaders would naturally prefer the informal control. After all, who would not prefer a method that makes few demands on his time yet yields the same results as troublesome, time-consuming methods? The eagerness of superiors to rely on informal control thus reinforces the tendencies of personnel at lower levels to handle their own problems. Whatever the benefits, however, one consequence is diminished information about subordinates.

AMBIGUOUS ALARMS

Yet another limitation of any feedback system is that the alarms are much more likely to go off when people are denied what they request than when their requests are granted. But subordinate noncompliance with agency policies may err on the side of excessive generosity as well as excessive severity. Infrequent warnings of noncompliance therefore may not mean subordinates are complying; it may mean only that their departures from policy pronouncements are chiefly of the lenient kind. Total absence of alarms would itself constitute a form of feedback, a warning that clients are *too* satisfied with the way personnel at lower levels are handling their jobs and that the tolerances for subordinate discretion may be excessively broad. Silence may therefore be just as informative as a constant clatter of alarm signals. Between these extremes, however, the import of some kinds of feedback may be hard to discern.

After all, different combinations of subordinate noncompliance can produce an "average" sounding of alarms. Such an average might appear if some subordinates are consistently too severe while others are just as consistently too lenient. It might develop if there were a regular bias against or in favor of some clients while all others are treated normally. It could emerge because many offended people have given up trying to obtain redress. If leaders rely heavily on the volume of feedback alarms to alert them to subordinate behavior, they can easily be misled into false security. In point of fact, however, the extent of the clamor is an index to which many leaders seem to attach great importance. To the extent they do not consciously try to probe beyond the norms, the usefulness of their administrative feedback systems is diluted.

THE PROBABILITIES OF UNDETECTED NONCOMPLIANCE

For all these reasons it is virtually certain that a great deal of subordinate noncompliance goes undetected in every organization. The built-in information gaps, the bounds of top-level receptivity, the fragmentation of headquarters, the effects of group solidarity, and the ambiguous implications of average volumes of alarm signals virtually assure this result.

What does it mean? Are the bureaus we studied in danger of falling prey to the hazardous consequences of noncompliance, or can their feedback systems safeguard them from this fate? Is the free play in the systems such that bureau headquarters are charged with responsibilities they cannot possibly fulfill, or are they, in spite of the limits of feedback, well aware of what their subordinates are up to? Can the feedback systems be adjusted to yield more complete data on subordinate behavior? Are the adjustments of such a character that a reasonably prudent man would consider them worth the costs?

V

Conclusions

OUR review of the operation of administrative feedback in the nine bureaus convinces us that if the leaders of any of the agencies fail to detect any persistent, pronounced, or widespread patterns of noncompliance on the part of their subordinates, it is not because of any breakdown of administrative feedback or because such patterns are inherently undetectable at headquarters. The leaders have the means at hand to keep track of what goes on below, and these means currently produce enough data in seven of the nine cases to disclose such behavior if the leaders want to know about it.

But it should not be taken for granted that leaders *do* want to know all about subordinate noncompliance. There are not only reasons why they are not inspired to seek out such knowledge; there are some incentives impelling them to *avoid* it. This incentive structure seems to us to have as much to do with the state of their information about subordinate behavior as do any characteristics of the administrative feedback systems.

It thus follows logically that if we should want to deepen and broaden leaders' knowledge of subordinate behavior, increasing the volume and variety of administrative feedback is not the indicated first step. Prior to that, it would be necessary to change the leaders' incentives to inform themselves about their subordinates. Otherwise, the added information would simply go the way of the current information.

NONCOMPLIANCE IS DETECTABLE

Despite the limits of feedback, it seems to us that the leaders of seven of the nine bureaus we studied are in a good position to determine what their subordinates are doing. The sources and kinds of data flowing back can be checked against each other to uncover misrepresentation, and the multiplicity of channels reduces the probabilities that interruptions or distortions of information flow will leave the leadership groups entirely at the mercy of unverifiable, self-serving allegations of subordinates about administrative behavior.

The feedback systems are far from foolproof. They are not total; in none of the agencies can leaders claim to know everything going on everywhere in their organizations, nor could they reasonably aspire to such omniscience through the current systems. It is therefore possible for minor deviations from policy pronouncements to continue for long periods without detection, and for individual cases of extreme deviation to occur from time to time. Having examined nine bureaus in some detail, we doubt that any large organization can avoid these hazards. Perhaps that is why some of the failures we noted in Chapter 1 occurred; those failures, as far as we can see from our study, are not tips of an iceberg of misinformation or absent information. All the shortcomings and problems of administrative feedback notwithstanding, the systems generally produce enough to serve the purposes of most leaders desirous of checking on the work of their subordinates.

Of course, just because the headquarters of most of our bureaus *can* figure out from the information available to them what is happening in the lower ranks, it does not follow the leaders *do* know what is going on. We would conjecture that the leaders of seven of the bureaus do in fact know a great deal about subordinate behavior. If any are grossly uninformed, it is not because the information required to correct their condition is not within their grasp any time they care to reach for it.

NEGATIVE MOTIVATIONS

Much writing on management embodies implicit assumptions that leaders of organizations are always eager to know what their subordinates are doing and therefore welcome all intelligence carrying information about their activities. But a contrary assumption is also plausible: there are reasons why they may prefer *not* to seek irrefutable evidence of the whole truth.

Avoiding Penalties

Americans subscribe simultaneously to two contradictory doctrines of responsibility for offenses. One is that no person should be punished for acts committed by someone else unless the first person directed the action or at least knew it was to be taken, knew it was an offense, and did nothing to stop it. The other is that superiors in hierarchies are or ought to be punishable for offenses committed by their subordinates except when the subordinates act in violation of orders from above.

If a pattern of offenses by subordinates is disclosed and it is also revealed that evidence of the pattern was close at hand for leaders who cared to inquire, the leaders can hardly make a plausible claim of ignorance. At the minimum, the data would constitute proof that they did nothing to stop what they knew was improper. At worst, the failure to prevent improprieties could be construed as sanctioning them. Instead of having a credible claim that they, too, were victimized, the leaders would be on the defensive against the charge that they were accomplices.

In fact, without realizing it and without benefiting personally, they may *be* accomplices. They may resort to the strategy of discouraging feedback about administrative behavior because they privately *approve* of the behavior they know they should, according to law and morality, prevent. They may secretly applaud harsher action than is formally allowed, or they may delight in lax enforcement of some standards. The temptations to establish claims of ignorance are as great when one is truly an accomplice as when one is really a victim.

Obviously, this does not mean all leaders try to cut themselves off from most knowledge about their subordinates; after all, one has to know a great deal to realize when it might be advantageous to restrict administrative feedback. What it implies is that there are times and circumstances in which leaders will indicate they would rather not learn more.

There are costs to such a strategy. Voluntary restrictions of administrative feedback increase the chances that some things will take place that the leaders would want to prevent if they knew about them. Moreover, subordinates who are aware their leaders will share their fate must exhibit far more loyalty, morale, obedience, and initiative than those who understand their superiors will abandon them.

Nevertheless, the incentives to pay these costs are strong, and what seem to be "failures" of feedback in some cases may well be the results of deliberate leadership choice.

Other Priorities

Leaders may choose not to concentrate much of the time and energy of their offices on tracking subordinate behavior for a second reason: other activities may well strike them as more important. Formulating policy, introducing innovation, expanding jurisdiction, winning greater authority and appropriations, standing off challenges by other interests and agencies, performing ritual and ceremonial functions, and representing the organization to higher headquarters and to Congress are also among their responsibilities. To be sure, all of these responsibilities can be jeopardized by massive noncompliance by subordinates. But when administrators have to choose among all these dangers and opportunities, subordinate noncompliance will not often appear at the head of the list unless it reaches crisis proportions. Balancing risks and potential benefits, therefore, command levels will often elect to give higher priority to other administrative concerns. If all hazards were equally probable and costly, if resources of all kinds were infinite, and if all the tasks of administration were equally pleasant and rewarding, presumably leadership resources would be more or less evenly divided among them. In the real world, orders of priority must be established, and surveying administrative feedback carefully will often be outranked by competing demands.

Resignation

A third reason leaders may not do as much with their existing or potential administrative feedback as they theoretically could is that some of them become resigned to the limits of their ability to alter the behavior of their subordinates. Why intensify the proofs of noncompliance if there is little you can do about it? Instead, why not intervene only when disasters or other crises oblige you to, and when they strengthen your hand? We do not mean to suggest the common attitude of organizational leaders is that they are helpless. But it is probably a rare leader who does not decide there are some activities or attributes of his subordinates he will overlook because he is not likely to have much effect on them and the attempt is therefore not worth the effort. The administrative feedback that monitors such behavior therefore exerts but a small claim on his interest.

Subordinate noncompliance with the wishes of leaders in large organizations is, as we noted earlier, virtually inevitable. Instructions from above are only one of many conflicting sets of factors that influence the behavior of subordinates. Often subordinates decline to comply fully with orders from above because they subscribe to values and perceptions that clash with the orders, or they belong to groups whose interests would be injured by compliance, or they disagree with the soundness of the orders. Sometimes they find it impossible to do what they are told to, and they therefore follow their own instincts. Prevention of all noncompliance is thus an unattainable ideal.

There may be leaders in some organizations determined to overcome these obstacles and obtain almost total compliance. It seems far more common for leaders to give up on some types of noncompliance, and to ignore feedback reporting on it. Resignation eats away at motivation.

Restricted Jurisdiction

The two agencies (both operating intergovernmental programs) whose feedback does not come up to the standard of the other seven had still another incentive to avoid feedback: at the time our study was made, they deliberately eschewed institution of detailed administrative feedback processes in order to avoid lending even a shred of credibility to the possible allegation that they infringed on state and local autonomy by checking closely on the recipients of the funds they distributed. The enabling statutes for these agencies explicitly declared their functions—education and law enforcement—to be state and local governmental responsibilities.[1] The long, bitter battles over federal aid to education had turned in large measure on fears of federal control, and the agencies were sensitized to these concerns. So the relative paucity of feedback in these instances does not indicate a collapse of feedback systems, and is not at odds with the evidence in the other seven cases; the nonconforming cases are products of prevailing motivations and conscious decision.

A STRATEGY FOR IMPROVEMENT

Why strive for improvement if the existing feedback about subordinate behavior seems in the main to provide sufficient information to apprise leaders adequately if they want to know what goes on below? Our specimen agencies work much as common lore holds they do and should. To be sure, modest changes here and there might make marginal improvements in the efficiency of information collection, transmission, or analysis, but with larger, more pressing problems crying out for attention, why devote time and talent and energy, not to mention other scarce resources, to a process that seems to function reasonably well? Why bother when, despite the limits of feedback and the incentives for leaders to restrict their knowledge of subordinate behavior, organizations

1. "Nothing contained in this Act shall be construed to authorize any department, agency, officer, or employee of the United States to exercise any direction, supervision, or control over the curriculum, program of instruction, administration, or personnel of any educational institution or school system." Sec. 604, Elementary and Secondary Education Act of 1965 (79 Stat. 57). See also Sec. 422 of the 1970 Amendments to the Elementary and Secondary Education Act of 1965 (84 Stat. 169).

"Congress finds further that crime is essentially a local problem that must be dealt with by State and local governments if it is to be controlled effectively." Declarations and Purpose, Omnibus Crime Control and Safe Streets Act of 1968 (82 Stat. 197).

manage to endure, democracy goes on its inevitably imperfect way, and feedback generally works successfully enough to forestall a breakdown in leadership and subversion of public policy?[2]

Improvements are worth the trouble they take because unseen injustice may still be done to many people and dissatisfactions may fester in the small areas of subordinate behavior not monitored. That the injustices and resulting discontents may not be gross enough to foster general rebellion should not be permitted to obscure the fact that democratic principles are being eroded. Nor should the belief that defects of policy may be responsible for most of the bitterness be accepted as justification of defects in administrative processes caused by top-level misapprehension of what happens at lower levels. If injustice can be corrected in even a small measure, if grievances that would otherwise be overlooked can be redressed to even a small degree, if avoidable unhappiness can be abated to just a small extent, remedies are worth considering. It is by no means self-evident that such irritants are so distributed in the population that relief for one set of people must inevitably produce equal distress for others. We think net increments of social and individual benefit are possible, often at modest cost, simply by bettering administrative feedback.

These benefits thus merit attention on grounds of principle. Because small irritants, like grains of sand in an eye or even in a shoe, may arouse discomfort out of all proportion to the source, they merit attention on strategic grounds as well. Improvements in feedback, though they promise no dramatic and sweeping changes, should not be regarded as trivial.

Some of the injustices and discontents develop in areas of leadership tolerance of subordinate discretion that feedback systems do not monitor. Some arise from the limited receptivity of top levels to the information about subordinates produced by administrative feedback. In both cases it is possible that leaders, if they were better informed, would disapprove of some things that go on at lower levels and would take corrective steps. But since they believe

2. See pp. 4–5, above.

—with reason—they would know if subordinates were wildly out of line, they are content with the information they already have, which may hide behavior unacceptable to them in principle. This condition is built into present arrangements.

Conceivably, noncompliance by subordinates may occasionally provide justice and redress of grievances that official policies preclude. On the whole, however, we assume the chances of justice being done in a democratic system of government are better if superiors know what their subordinates are doing than if they do not.

Since the principal source of the administrative feedback problem is not its volume or quality, the object of improvement efforts should be to induce leaders to make more effective use of the existing information rather than to add to the flow of data into headquarters. As things stand, additional flow would not have much effect on leaders' behavior. In other words, restructuring the system of incentives seems to hold greater promise than multiplying the details received by headquarters.

In fact, the volume of raw material flowing to headquarters suggests that *reducing* rather than increasing the volume of information about subordinate behavior might improve feedback. There is a tendency for reporting requirements that originated for reasons that have disappeared into the mists of history to continue because it takes more effort to discontinue them than to let them roll on. Reporting requirements are like the contents of attics— accumulations always in need of cleaning out.

Furthermore, multiplying feedback means intensified surveillance of subordinates, a practice that can make the climate of administration worse instead of better. People placed in a position where someone is always looking over their shoulders may respond with hostility or excessive caution or both. In an environment of mutual confidence and trust—typified by grants of broad discretion and by minimal surveillance—subordinates may make strenuous efforts to comply in order to sustain the congenial milieu and the expression of confidence that such delegations imply. They are also freer to improvise in order to achieve the *intent* of their directives instead of merely obeying the letter of the law.

Ultimately, therefore, their behavior may be more efficient and effective and considerate and just than it would be if they were less motivated, less imaginative, and more "correct."

For example, if large numbers of routine decisions trip feedback alarms because tolerance limits have been narrowed, subordinates are likely to begin to refer many cases to higher levels for action instead of taking responsibility themselves. Consequently, reaching decisions on even routine matters can begin to take longer and longer with little demonstrable change in quality, while supervisors are in effect reduced by the rising burden of clearance and review from performing the tasks of management to doing the work of their subordinates.

Or subordinates will begin to interpret the standing orders and rulebooks of their organizations in the most literal sense. No organization can operate under these conditions, a peculiarity seldom discussed in management literature; a certain degree of noncompliance is apparently essential to effective administration, and labor slowdowns by meticulous observation of all the rules have now become familiar tactics in industrial relations. Intensified feedback may well be construed by subordinates as evidence their superiors do not have much confidence in them, and they may respond by cleaving ever more strictly to narrow (and therefore safe) interpretations of their guidelines. Such literalness may not help an agency's program, but it protects the individual employee when every action is subject to scrutiny from above.

Once a climate is established in which organization members try to divest themselves of both responsibility and discretion, everybody tends to grow defensive for fear fellow workers will saddle him with blame for errors or for unhappy consequences of technically proper acts. Instead of cooperation and mutual support, maneuvering and Byzantine politics become the order of the day; energies and skills that would otherwise go into organizational output are channeled into internal warfare.

So intensifying surveillance of subordinates would not be the most promising way of trying to improve administrative feedback even if it were directed at the real cause of noncompliance. But it is *not* directly on target because it is not aimed at what appears to be the chief problem of administrative feedback—the curious structure of incentives that impels agencies' headquarters not to take full advantage of the information flows already at their disposal. Insofar as improvement is called for, the best place to look for it is in the domain of incentives.

CHANGING HEADQUARTERS' INCENTIVES

Trying to change nonpecuniary incentives is an exceedingly difficult undertaking; it requires modification of the behavior and values of large numbers of people in the face of habit, vested interests, and the prevailing system of rewards and deprivations. Still, even a single voice calling persistently for change can sometimes effect major transformations. The quest is not hopeless even though the odds against success are heavy.

Redefining Leadership Responsibility

One approach would be to abandon the fiction that leaders, at least up to the bureau level, are by virtue of ignorance untainted by patterns of noncompliance with their announced policies. Our impression is that absence of feedback is not one of the reasons for their ignorance. Hence, it would not be unfair to hold leaders responsible for the actions of their subordinates, thereby neutralizing their motivations to neglect some of the information now within their grasp.

Such a position presents dilemmas. It would oblige the superiors of bureau leaders, for example, to try to determine whether subordinate actions acknowledged by everyone to violate bureau standards constitute the kind of persistent pattern that prevailing administrative feedback can detect or, contrariwise, are unique events that the leaders could not be expected to know about in time to prevent them. But whenever responsibilities are allocated and fault is assigned, such decisions must be made. They are never easy. If leaders are not held accountable in this way, their inclination to overlook administrative feedback is reinforced.

Another dilemma of this position is that it increases the vulnerability of leaders to intimidation by their subordinates. Leaders are always more or less threatened by the possibilities of subordinate disobedience, but the threat is intensified if there is an augmented chance that the leaders will be implicated in the subordinate action instead of totally disjoined. If leaders victimized by administrative sabotage are adjudged as guilty as the perpetrators, all leaders may recoil from any actions that might antagonize lower levels, thus weakening instead of strengthening control. A boomerang effect is a distinct possibility.

Defining leadership responsibility more broadly in order to encourage fuller use of administrative feedback may also persuade some of the people whom governments would like to attract to public service that the risks are disproportionately high. To be sure, it may also induce people who *shrink* from responsibility to reject such positions, and to that extent would be salutary. As the history of civil service reform makes clear, however, the unanticipated effects of change can be quite extensive, a problem not to be ignored when considering proposals for administrative change.

It is disquieting to punish one person for the acts of another on the grounds that the first person *could* have known, had he made the proper effort, what the second was doing and therefore should at least have *tried* to stop it. Though such assertions are discomforting, there *is* evidence that administrative feedback does produce enough information about subordinate behavior to render the assertions credible. If it seems necessary to stimulate leaders to attend more closely to administrative feedback than prevailing incentives motivate them to, the discomfort is worth bearing.

On balance, we do not regard the dilemmas as fatal. We believe that redefinition of leadership responsibility, carried out with restraint, would do much more good than harm. In operational terms, it would mean that discovery of persistent patterns of noncompliance in any organization should lead to inquiries into the performance of current *and of past* leaders, not just of lower officers, and certainly not merely of the rank and file. We think the risks involved are worth taking.

Increasing External Evaluation

If leaders knew that many people outside their organizations were almost as able as they to judge accurately whether or not their subordinates were complying with headquarters policies, it seems likely the headquarters staffs would be moved to make more use of administrative feedback and to resist the negative incentives to which they are exposed. It is one thing to indicate you did not, and could not possibly, know of noncompliance when no one is in a good position to refute you. It is quite another thing when outsiders can demonstrate that *they*, even without the informational advantages enjoyed by leaders, were aware of the noncompliance; dubious alibis will not stand up.

It is not easy for most outsiders, even if they are the superiors of bureau leaders, to determine whether personnel at the lower levels of bureaus are doing what the leaders want done. Outsiders do not ordinarily acquire the familiarity with the standing orders and manuals of the bureaus that insiders develop as a matter of course. Most outsiders do not enjoy the personal contacts and formal training of insiders. Most are not paid to devote full time to overseeing the work of any individual bureau. Access to official documents has been broadened by statute in the federal government, but for an outsider to piece together a picture of subordinate behavior is still an arduous business. External evaluation of subordinate behavior is thus no simple matter. The external channels we studied turned out to bear very little information useful in evaluation.

Resolute, well-organized interest groups are potentially capable of evaluating subordinate performance, and some of them do. Often, however, they are so identified with the bureaus in their fields that they share the interests and perspectives of the leaders. Anyway, they tend to concentrate on broad policy issues rather than on subordinate compliance; when they, like congressmen and political parties, provide "case work" for constituents, they address only isolated cases. Since the best-equipped outsiders rarely question patterns of subordinate behavior, and other outsiders are not usually able to, they furnish bureau leaders with few incentives to delve more deeply and consistently into available data on subordinate behavior; not even wider access to government records under the Freedom of Information Act seems to have made much difference. If outside surveillance is to serve as a stimulus, many outsiders will have to alter their own behavior and priorities first and give as much attention to administrative detail as to policy pronouncements, statutes, and general regulations.

Units and agencies inside government can also serve as detached observers. The administrative levels above the bureaus, for example, already possess enough discretion (though perhaps not enough resources) to increase their autonomous inquiries—especially inspections—into subordinate behavior in the bureaus. Indeed, the capability has been demonstrated in some instances: the Department of Agriculture, for instance, has an inspector general; the Department of Health, Education, and Welfare has an Audit Agency that construes its mission broadly; the Federal Aviation Administration has an Office of Appraisal that performs similarly. The General Accounting Office, especially under its new leadership, has interpreted its role as a managerial one rather than as a bookkeeping audit exclusively. The impact of the work of these bodies indicates how much can be accomplished by existing organizations without grand changes in organizational design. It also suggests that some larger changes, such as the introduction of ombudsmen into the administrative establishment, may help induce bureau leaders to elevate attention to subordinate behavior in their own hierarchies of priorities.

Much can be done by interests outside the bureaus even if present arrangements are left pretty much as they are. The effectiveness of outsiders could be magnified many times if a type of information about subordinate behavior that is not now available for the most part, even within bureaus, were to be gathered and disseminated by the government: clients' perceptions of what subordinates actually do. Survey research could provide these fresh data and insights.

Survey Research on Subordinate Behavior

Survey research is probably best known for its inquiries into people's attitudes and preferences and evaluations and beliefs with regard to policies, products, individuals, and organizations (usually political parties). But it also yields information on what the respondents have actually *done*—whether they voted in a given election, for example, what products and services they bought and used, what parties they belong to, and so on. Both kinds of inquiry could be employed in organizations to find out what subordinates do and how their behavior is perceived by those who come in contact with the organizations.

Interviews with samples of agency clienteles could be aimed, for instance, at discovering how long clients had to wait for service, what was done for them, how long they spent with the persons serving them, whether product inspectors appeared personally at work sites, what they did while on the site, whether the service was judged to be courteous and helpful, and so on. These dimensions of the relationship between the people inside organizations and those outside are scarcely touched by the modes of feedback that currently provide most of the information to headquarters about subordinate behavior.

To be sure, clients and others who do business with public agencies do not lack for channels through which to voice their complaints, and a good many dissatisfactions and criticisms are indeed expressed through existing channels; there are many forms of such participation in the administrative process. But nothing in these channels indicates whether the complainants are typical or are exceptions; there is no way of knowing if they speak for a large number of people who share their sentiments and perceptions (but lack the confidence or initiative or sophistication or hopefulness to articulate their views) or if they speak for themselves alone. Even furnishing postpaid cards or questionnaires to every individual with whom an organization has contact does not quiet this doubt, although it does reduce it. There are still thresholds of inertia, ignorance, suspicion, and despair to be overcome before people take advantage of such ballots, which means it is impossible to know from the returns whether there is a large body of people who have simply given up even though they are not properly served. Moreover, since most people who consider themselves properly served will not take the trouble to return notices, there will be few favorable returns. So feedback from self-selected respondents exclusively is only a crude index of gross discontent. As indicators of what subordinates are doing, communications from people sufficiently motivated to volunteer their views leave much to be desired. Survey research escapes these handicaps.

We do not believe, however, that surveys should be conducted by members of the bureaus themselves. After all, the survey research findings would merely add to their feedback, and they are not motivated to use all the feedback they already have. If the purpose is to change their incentives to use feedback about subordinate compliance, it is likelier to come about if the surveys are carried out and reported by teams outside the bureaus.

If research were located outside the bureaus to which it applied, the results would be far less suspect—and, in fact, less susceptible to manipulation for the bureau's own purposes. It would be hard enough to keep concerned interests from tampering with the findings no matter where the studies are conducted; it would be almost impossible to prevent some doctoring of the results by researchers whose paychecks come from and careers lie in the bureaus to which their research is addressed. Certainly, under these conditions, it would be difficult to persuade most people the results were not doctored to some degree, even if they were not. If inquiries of this kind into subordinate behavior in the bureaus are to be wholly reliable and accurate and above suspicion, they clearly ought not to be done by the bureaus.

Indeed, they probably ought to be done outside the departments and agencies in which the bureaus are lodged, for the same reason. The people who perform the service should be as immune as possible from the pressures that everyone with a stake in the findings is sure to bring to bear on the research. While a comparably sensitive operation by the Bureau of Labor Statistics suggests it is not impossible to attain a reasonably high level of insulation within a regular department, the prospects for doing so seem brighter in a more autonomous setting. In fact, a location outside the executive branch as a whole would not be amiss, either in a new organization created for the purpose or perhaps within the General Accounting Office, whose title belies its broadened concept of its responsibilities. Or perhaps the service could be purchased from commercial operators.

The location is not crucial in and of itself; the protection of the new organ's *independence* is what counts. Any arrangement that endows it with adequate authority, personnel, funding, and self-direction (subject only to intervention by congressional, presidential, or judicial authority in extraordinary circumstances to prevent abuses of power) is probably as good as any other. A separate and strong location would conduce to this status.

The findings of the survey research organization must be made public if they are to have the intended effect. If bureau leaders' superiors, competitors, critics, and the general public are provided with indexes of the extent to which the bureaus' subordinates comply with directives, obviously the bureaus themselves will be less inclined to ignore the more complete information already flowing into their offices. Failure to publish the information gathered by survey research would mean relinquishing a most powerful instrument for changing the incentives of bureau headquarters' staffs.

We can see many reasons for proceeding cautiously—on a small-scale, experimental basis—with a program of this kind. Survey research is expensive, and more should be known about the ratio of the costs to the returns before it is undertaken on a sweeping scale to gauge subordinate compliance with policy. Defining populations to sample will not be easy; including or excluding some groups will make a big difference in how subordinate behavior is portrayed. Distinguishing respondents' descriptions rooted in knowledge and experience from portrayals based on hearsay or even on unfounded belief may present serious problems. Nevertheless, we think a limited experiment is worth trying. Survey research is now sufficiently developed to solve some of these problems, and judgments about the benefits, whether negative or affirmative, are sheer conjecture at this point. The potential seems promising enough to justify a modest investment in an appraisal.

PRESSING ON

The short-run consequences of improving administrative feedback are likely to be limited but important. The long-run consequences could be quite far-reaching. One result of shortcomings in the feedback process is that discrepancies between the intentions of leaders and the behavior of subordinates are likely to increase with time because each such discrepancy tends to engender and exculpate others. With large organizations playing ever larger roles in modern society, the cumulative impact of imperceptible divergences of this kind, even if each individual divergence is singly of little significance, can shake the foundations of public administrative structures and democratic principles.

Perhaps challenges of this character must reach urgent proportions before remedial measures can win much support; crisis is a powerful stimulus to action. But the responses to crisis are often hasty and extreme. Time to experiment and to fashion appropriate instruments to improve administrative feedback is a luxury we now enjoy. It would be a pity to waste it.

Improving feedback within bureaus, however, would be only the beginning. Although we gathered no data on practices and problems at higher levels, there are reasons to suspect that knowledge about the administrative behavior of rank and file is sparser in the ranks above bureau headquarters than in bureau headquarters. Departments, after all, encompass dozens of bureaus and are also further removed from the field. And the responsibilities of the White House are yet broader and more remote. It would therefore not be surprising if administrative feedback to the top echelons were found to be in greater need of attention than feedback in the bureaus. The importance of such a finding for democratic government would be immense. Inquiry should not stop with the bureaus.

Every researcher ends his report with a plea for further research. These entreaties often arise from the special curiosity of the researchers rather than from the broader social implications of the additional knowledge. We are impressed with how many assumptions about the functioning of our governmental system rest in the last analysis on untested faith in feedback as one crucial component of that system. Just suppose that faith is misplaced.

Bibliographical Note

Administrative Feedback Generally

What we have here labeled "administrative feedback" has not often been studied empirically. Walter Gellhorn's *When Americans Complain: Governmental Grievance Procedures* (Cambridge: Harvard University Press, 1966) is probably the broadest treatment of some problems of administrative feedback. Harold L. Wilensky's *Organizational Intelligence: Knowledge and Policy in Government and Industry* (New York: Basic Books, 1967), though more concerned with substantive than administrative feedback, also examines evidence on a wide array of difficulties. See also David J. Olson, "Citizen Grievance Letters as a Gubernatorial Control Device in Wisconsin," *Journal of Politics*, Vol. 31 (August 1969); John D. C. Little, Chandler H. Stevens, and Peter Tropp, "Citizen Feedback System: The Puerto Rico Model," *National Civic Review*, Vol. 60 (April 1971).

Public Reporting

The public reporting practices of governmental agencies once attracted the attention of scholars; see Herman C. Beyle, *Governmental Reporting in Chicago* (Chicago: University of Chicago Press, 1928), and *Public Reporting* (Chicago: Municipal Administrative Service, 1931). But these studies do not review the methods by which agency leaders are informed of subordinate behavior; thus they are relevant only as distant historical antecedents of this inquiry.

Legal Studies

A number of legal studies have explored the extent of compliance by lower courts (and also by other officials and by private citizens) with the decisions of higher courts; see, for example, Walter Murphy, "Lower Court Checks on Supreme Court Power," *American Political Science Review*, Vol. 53 (December 1959). See also Gordon Patric, "The Impact of a Court Decision: Aftermath of the McCollum Case," *Journal of Public Law*, Vol. 6 (1957); Ellis Katz, "Patterns of Compliance with the Schempp

Decision," *Journal of Public Law*, Vol. 14 (1965); William K. Muir, Jr., *Prayer in the Public Schools: Law and Attitude Change* (Chicago: University of Chicago Press, 1967); Richard M. Johnson, *The Dynamics of Compliance: Supreme Court Decision-Making from a New Perspective* (Evanston, Ill.: Northwestern University Press, 1967); Gary Orfield, *The Reconstruction of Southern Education: The Schools and the 1964 Civil Rights Act* (New York: Wiley, 1969); and Fred Wirt, *Politics of Southern Equality: Law and Social Change in a Mississippi County* (Chicago: Aldine, 1970).

The way administration of criminal justice diverges from procedures established in law has also received attention; see, for instance, Wayne LaFave, *Arrest: The Decision to Take a Suspect into Custody* (Boston: Little, Brown, 1965); Michael S. Wald and others, "Interrogations in New Haven: The Impact of *Miranda*," *Yale Law Journal*, Vol. 76 (July 1967); and U.S. Commission on Civil Rights, *Law Enforcement: A Report on Equal Protection in the South* (Washington: Government Printing Office, 1965).

A panel at the 1971 meeting of the American Political Science Association was devoted to compliance with judicial decisions; see Bradley C. Canon, "Reactions of State Supreme Courts to a U.S. Supreme Court Civil Liberties Decision"; Alan H. Schechter, "The Impact of Open Housing Laws on Suburban Realtors"; and Alan M. Sager, "The Impact of Supreme Court Loyalty Oath Decisions" (papers presented at the meeting; processed).

A good anthology on the subject is Theodore L. Becker, *The Impact of Supreme Court Decisions* (New York: Oxford University Press, paperback, 1968). An extensive annual bibliography has been carried in *Law and Society Review* since 1968 and a bibliography (with respect to the criminal sanction only) appears in William J. Chambliss, *Crime and the Legal Process* (New York: McGraw-Hill, 1969).

Feedback and Administration

A host of volumes deals generally with feedback control, and some of its applications to management, such as Preston P. Le Breton, *Administrative Intelligence-Information Systems* (Boston: Houghton Mifflin, 1969); and Richard W. Brightman, *Information Systems for Modern Management* (New York: Macmillan, 1971). But they tend to offer the authors' conclusions, not empirical evidence. An exception is Thomas L. Whisler, *Information Technology and Organizational Change* (Belmont, Calif.: Wadsworth, 1970), which also contains a comprehensive set of references.

Paucity of Data

Aside from these scattered, diverse materials, we could find nothing analyzing, or even describing, actual experience with administrative feedback in live organizations. Conceivably, a careful survey of case studies of organizations, and of controlled experiments with organizations, might yield incidental data illuminating the subject. It appears to us, however, that most of what is said and written about the means by which administrators are informed of subordinate behavior, and of the relative effectiveness of the various means, has hitherto been based on assumptions rarely tested against actual performance.